D1084270

I'm Trying to Sit at His Feet, but Who's Going to Cook Dinner?

I'm Trying to Sit at His Feet, but Who's Going to Cook Dinner?

Cathy Lechner

CREATION HOUSE
BOOKS ABOUT SPIRIT-LED LIVING
ORLANDO, FLORIDA

Creation House
Strang Communications Company
600 Rinehart Road
Lake Mary, FL 32746
Phone: 407-333-3132
Fax: 407-333-7100
Web site: http://www.creationhouse.com

*I lovingly dedicate this book to my "Boaz,"
my beloved husband, Randi.*

Acknowledgments

I will forever be grateful to the following people. They love me — the good, the bad and everything in between.

My precious children, Jerusha, Hannah, Gabriel, Samuel and Abagael.

Erin, what would I have ever done without you? You are more than a secretary — you are my forever friend.

To my awesome and patient parents, Clive and Rose Rothert, for all the hours spent typing and editing, and the months you gave up your ministry in order to serve mine. Only the Lord knows your sacrifice.

To my wonderful pastors at New Covenant Ministries, Wiley and Jeana Tomlinson, who speak faith and truth, much of what is found in this book — you are the best pastors in the world!

For my grandmother, Ruth, whose eighty-eight years of life, prayers and godly example have kept me through the darkest times.

To our wonderful staff of Covenant Ministries, who selflessly give to build the kingdom of our Lord Jesus: Trudy Cooper, Mark Cooper, Eric and Lynn Jones, and Laura Lee O'Toole.

To Stephen and Joy Strang and the staff of Creation House who saw in me something I couldn't see and made a dream come true.

Most of all, I give glory and honor to my Lord Jesus Christ. He loves me, keeps me and gives me life.

Contents

Introduction

I Want to Be Spiritual, but I Can't Remember the Words to Scripture Songs

---

Put your heads down and put the tarp over you," the Filipino pastor yelled from the front seat. Quickly, my daughter Jerusha and I laid down on the floor and covered up. The only sound I heard were the rocks under the tires of the speeding truck and the sound of my pounding heart.

This was not at all what I had imagined some months earlier when a letter arrived asking me to come and minister at a pastors' conference on the island of Mindanao, Philippines.

After a four-day conference, we were to travel to a coastal city to hold a crusade and encourage the local churches. The pastor told us he had received a threat earlier the same day from Muslims stating two Americans would be murdered. Well, there were only four of us: my mother, my father, my daughter and myself. I briefly thought, "My parents have lived a good, full life. What better way to go than as a martyr for the kingdom." The pastors placed us in separate vehicles as we headed out for the conference. Lying under that tarp, I was very aware of the danger we were in as the Muslims lay waiting for us.

I thought to myself, "Was it only morning I sat in the light of the sun under a mosquito net, weeping and worshipping the Lord?" It seemed like a lifetime ago I heard the Holy Spirit whisper sweetly, "Daughter, you are safe. You are as safe in the middle of the journey as you are when you arrive."

In a whispered voice I asked my daughter if she was afraid. "Of course not," she replied in full voice. "The Lord brought in the money to send me, and I am going to minister with you. Besides that, all my prophecies have not been fulfilled, so I can't die yet." Whispering again, I assured her "I'm not afraid either. I was just checking on you." Talk about calling "things that are not as though they were!" (Rom. 4:17, NIV).

We made it through. In fact, over and over in my life I've made it through. This book doesn't have enough pages to recount the times my back was against the wall. Whether it was physically, emotionally or spiritually — my God always brought me through.

Where did the hope come from to go on? Getting at my Lord's feet is where the strength comes from. Pouring out my heart in love, telling Him how much I trust Him even when I don't understand everything I am called to walk through. In return, He gives me strength, joy and victory to face the test.

The ministry the Lord has graciously given to me is of a prophetic nature. That is, knowledge of the heart and mind of God that *He* speaks into my spirit to share with an individual, a couple or a congregation. With that gift comes a strong anointing to break the yokes of bondage many precious Christians are under. Traveling throughout the world I've seen literally thousands of people encouraged by the "word of the Lord."

I am also a wife and a mother. A very busy mother, with a teenager and four children two years of age and younger!

The pressure, distractions and the cares of this life will try to push out the very thing that is our source of life. Being in His presence is not an option. Exercising the principles laid out in this book are not a luxury — they are a necessity. I would end up at "Happy Acres" doing basket weaving if it were not for the secret place of the Most High. In fact, it's the only place my children can't find me.

Dear Reader, I have been where you have been (or are right now). It may not be the exact place or the same circumstance, but I know what it's like to fight fear. I've lived through rejection and betrayal from people who said they would love me forever and learned the secret of not becoming bitter.

I have faced infertility, church splits and pet deaths. The seeming unfairness and injustice was overwhelming. I have known plenty and I have lived in poverty. Through it all my love and trust in Jesus has grown. My anger at the enemy knows no bounds. I have almost lost my marriage, and I've seen God totally restore my bruised and broken heart.

You have not received this book by accident — it's a divine appointment. With God's anointing, these printed words have life, hope and power in them. The anointing of the Holy Spirit has prepared this divine appointment in answer to your heart's hungry cry.

We are going to laugh together, cry together, but God is going to set you free and release joy within you, my friend. Are you ready?

1

I'm Trying to Sit at His Feet, but Who's Going to Cook Dinner?

Don't you just love it when your husband calls and says, "By the way, we're having company for dinner tonight"?

It's bad enough when you get a phone call, but Martha was not so fortunate. The Word tells us,

> As Jesus and his disciples were on their way, he came to a village where a woman named Martha opened her home to him. She had a sister called Mary, who sat at the Lord's feet, listening to what he said. But

13

Martha was distracted by all the preparations that had to be made. She came to him and asked, "Lord, don't you care that my sister has left me to do the work by myself? Tell her to help me!"

"Martha, Martha," the Lord answered, "you are worried and upset about many things, but only one thing is needed. Mary has chosen what is better, and it will not be taken away from her" (Luke 10:38-42, NIV).

Many people have painted Martha as the not-so-spiritual woman. Even though she seems to get a bad rap, we know that if we didn't have Marthas, we wouldn't have as many wonderful conferences as we have today. The conferences would never get organized.

Martha had a spirit of hospitality, the ability to entertain. When the knock came at the door, she welcomed Jesus and His entourage. I can just see her running to the kitchen to see what she had in the cupboard to cook. No doubt she had a reputation in the village for being a gracious hostess, and she had to maintain that image.

Then there was Mary. All she wanted to do was sit at the Master's feet, listen to Him and be in His presence, which didn't go over too well with her sister Martha.

Earlier in the book of Luke, the story is told of a woman who took a precious alabaster box filled with perfumed oil and poured it over Jesus' feet. This woman was probably Mary. Those around her reprimanded her — this perfumed oil equaled at least a year's wages, and it represented a person's social security. As they could afford to, people added to the ointment and saved it to use or sell in their old age.

Martha was a true servant. No one had a home like she had; no one could make you feel more welcome than she could. She was always serving. Service is linked to work, and I think she felt her sister should be doing more of it.

I'm sure Mary helped around the house, went to the market and did all the things women did in those days, because if she didn't, we know Martha would have had plenty more to say to her.

The difference wasn't so much that Mary wasn't doing all the things Martha did. The difference was in attitude.

We can get so busy doing service that we become distracted. That's when we develop a bad attitude toward the very ones we are serving. There was no doubt that Martha was devoted and committed to Jesus. Wasn't she a good hostess? Didn't she open her home and serve Him every time He came to town?

Intimacy in Five Minutes?

Mary realized that serving wasn't as important as knowing. She made time to spend in the Lord's presence even when there were other "good" things to do. Most of us wish we were like Mary, but we find ourselves pulling a "Martha" instead.

We start our mornings intending to get into the presence of the Lord, and we feel guilty about our spiritual carelessness. Suddenly we discover it's too late, and we have to get ready for work. We jump in the car, race down the road singing, "I love you Jesus, and I lift my voice to You. Hallelujah! What's wrong with that driver? Can't he go any faster? Get out of my way! Oh yes, Jesus be with me today...honk, honk...I need Your protection." Sound familiar?

I wonder how you would feel if your husband came to you and said, "I've got ten minutes to get to work. Get in the car, and we'll have some intimacy on the way." Sounds silly, doesn't it? But isn't that how we often treat Jesus?

Some substitute a "good" Christian TV program for intimacy with God. Sort of a "third person." Then there are those who take advantage of their time in the shower, all five minutes of it.

When we have intimacy with Him, He wants our undivided attention — in our prayer closet, behind closed doors, just us and the Lord. You have heard it said that it's not how high you jump on Sunday, it's how straight you walk the rest of the week. Jesus told His disciples to enter their closet and shut the door. This means shut the doors of our busy lives, our self-wills and our circumstances. Intimacy in prayer cannot be realized until we enter the closet and shut the door.

I Don't Want to Blow It 'Cause I Hate Rebukes

Jesus really did love Martha and appreciated her servant's heart. However, Mary knew what it meant to worship and serve. Martha didn't know what it was like to sit at the feet of Jesus. She worried more about the dinner and the dishes.

Jesus rebuked Martha. He said, "Martha, Martha, you are worried and upset about many things, but only one thing is needed. Mary has chosen what is better, and it will not be taken from her." I believe He said it lovingly. Just because He corrects us, it doesn't mean He doesn't love us. The Word tells us that Jesus loved Martha and her sister and her brother. Notice that it didn't say, "Mary and her sister and brother."

I'm always amazed at the answers I get when I ask someone if they are a Christian. They tell me what church they attend and all the committees they serve on. All that is wonderful, but my question is, "How much time do you spend doing the important things, like sitting at His feet?"

The second thing that happened to Martha is that she got irritated. She lost her focus. The longer she worked around the house, the more frustrated she became.

You know how you react when you are irritated and you give everyone the silent treatment. You begin to slam stuff around, and the cabinet doors get a fervent banging. Some call it charismatic cursing.

Then someone asks you what's wrong and you say, between tight lips, "Nothing," which is an obvious lie. No one tries to destroy the cupboard doors if nothing is wrong.

Company's Coming, Get the Mop!

In one of my recent meetings, a woman came to me all agitated. She told me she needed prayer, but she had to be first because she had to get home to vacuum. "I always vacuum on Tuesdays, and I must get home because I can't get off my schedule." My first inclination was to tell her to get a life.

Some women have certain chores they do on particular days. My mother was like that. My parents pastored a small congregation, so my mother helped supplement their income by working outside the home. That meant come rain or come shine, the house had to be cleaned from top to bottom on Saturday. I hated Saturdays. My brothers always disappeared. And any time she knew company was coming, my dad said she felt she had to do spring cleaning. Thank God she's not like that anymore!

With this type of attitude problem, Martha proceeded to tell Jesus a thing or two. "How does Mary get by, sitting at Your feet while I do all the work?" She felt she wasn't appreciated; she thought, "He probably likes Mary better because she's so spiritual."

When we were pastoring, I occasionally worked in the church nursery. I always bought those little blue bags for soiled diapers, and I really got irritated when the workers would just wrap dirty diapers in a paper towel and toss them in the wastebasket. The problem was that the wastebaskets wouldn't be emptied until the following week when it was someone else's turn to clean the church. Sometimes, no one showed up to clean at all. The place smelled awful.

I guess I fell into the Martha category because I griped and complained and felt I wasn't appreciated. It was a service with no joy. We do reap what we sow. It really doesn't matter if anyone sees what we are doing, as long as we do it with joy.

I Could Stay Home and Be Miserable

I have seen women who think they could nag their husbands into the kingdom. They announce that they are going to church, and for the sake of the children, the least he could do is go with them. By the time they leave, they've worked themselves into a frenzy and are filled with anger. They slam the door on their way out to worship the Lord.

You can almost hear her husband saying, "Why should I go? I could be mad and depressed right here at home. I don't need what you say you have."

Then the Marthas are overcome by a feeling of isolation: I'm all alone in this; everyone wants the glory, but no one wants the work. What is your motive in doing the work of the Lord? Is it Christ-centered or Martha-directed?

After isolation comes vexation. It becomes an intolerable burden, and you become troubled, anxious and uptight. Everything has got to be done now!

I really am amused when I get into someone's car and they say, "Please excuse the mess, it's never like this." I think, You're not being truthful. It probably always looks like this, because mine does.

I have the same approach to housecleaning. My excuse is, I've been gone and I really haven't had time to do my spring cleaning. However, if you come back in December, it still looks the same, so I simply decide to wait until next spring.

A friend of mine was helping me with my housework and was late getting to my home. She told me she was late because she was washing her baseboards. I thought, "Baseboards, baseboards — do I have baseboards?"

I can imagine Martha being upset because Mary wouldn't come in the kitchen and help with the dishes. But I've learned the dishes can wait. After dinner one night with some friends, I offered to help with the dishes. "Don't worry about the dishes," my friend answered. "We'll just pile them up and I'll

do them later. I would rather have the fellowship instead."
That really blessed me, because I feel the same way when I
entertain.

I Have a Word for You

You want to spend time alone with the Lord on a daily
basis. You start out great, but then the phone rings, or you eye
the unmade beds, or you go to the refrigerator and it smells
like dead fish, so you feel you just have to clean it right now.
You become consumed with things other than the Lord, and
you cannot stop.

Unplug the phone, close your eyes to your housework for
that hour. You can always go back to those things. Time spent
with the Lord will enable you to do your Martha-directed
work even better.

When Lazarus died, Martha was really upset with Jesus. She
told Him that if He had come sooner, her brother would not
have died (see John 11:21).

But Jesus told her that if she only believed, she would see
the glory of the Lord. If she had spent more time at His feet,
instead of spending so much time in the kitchen, she wouldn't
have experienced such unbelief.

It's better to spend ten uninterrupted minutes in His presence every day than no minutes at all. Later, make up for lost
time and pray for an hour. I'm so familiar with the routine: I'll
just make one phone call first, and while I'm praying, I'll
throw a load of clothes in the washer and that chicken won't
thaw by supper time if I don't take it out of the freezer before
I pray...oops! The first load is done so I'll throw that load in
the dryer...oh well, I may as well start another load in the
washer. And it goes on and on until the kids get home from
school and your husband comes in and wants his supper. Next
day, more of the same.

Mary never said a word when her sister came in and got

upset with her. She didn't even rebuke Judas and the disciples when they criticized her for breaking the alabaster box and pouring out the perfume on Jesus. When you are sitting at Jesus' feet, looking into His eyes, nothing else matters.

When Lazarus died, Martha went to his grave to meet Jesus, ready to rebuke Him for not coming sooner. None of the other mourners went with her.

But when Martha hurried back to the house to tell her sister that Jesus was asking for her, Mary quickly ran out to meet Him — and the others followed her. I like to think that everyone knew what kind of person she was, a woman devoted to her Lord. And that's why they followed *her*.

When a woman becomes pregnant, eventually her belly will grow. When she walks into a room, everyone knows she has been intimate with a man. When you have spent time in the presence of the Lord, it will become evident to those around you that you have been with Him, because you have the fruit of the Spirit. You will be a joy to be around, and your joy will spill over onto your family.

When Mary arrived at the scene, she said the identical words that Martha said: "Lord, if You had been here, my brother would not have died." The only difference was that she fell at His feet (see John 11:32). She was able to worship in her agony.

In the face of adversity, many women pull away from God. They say they can't take it anymore, and they abort the vision He has given them just before the promise comes to pass. They are stuck in transition and make an inner vow never to trust again.

When Jesus saw Mary weeping, He was deeply moved in His spirit. The scriptures do not show Him reacting that way to Martha. Even though He loved Martha, it was Mary's tears that moved Him, because He saw her heart. She had been at His feet and was able to worship Him, even though she lost someone she dearly loved.

When He told the men to roll the stone away, Martha was filled with unbelief, but Mary didn't say a word. Because she had sat at His feet, she knew raising Lazarus from the dead was not too great a miracle for her Master to perform.

When Jesus returned to Martha's house, she was back in the kitchen, cooking and serving, while Mary poured expensive perfume on her Lord's feet and wiped it with her hair. That occurred shortly before His crucifixion. The perfume represented sacrifice; Jesus told her she was anointing Him for His death.

Service requires sacrifice. I cannot express the sorrow I feel when I leave Randi, my husband, and my children to board a plane to fulfill a speaking engagement. I try to think of Mary, and how she sacrificed the very thing she had been saving for herself when she poured the ointment over Jesus' feet. When Mary and her family returned from witnessing Jesus' crucifixion, I'm sure the aroma of that ointment still filled the room. Our desire should be that long after we leave, the aroma of His presence so fills the room that others will know we have spent time at Jesus' feet.

The Word says what Mary did will be remembered. Will you be remembered for the good dinner you cooked, or how well you entertained your Sunday school class? Those are good things.

As for me, I want to be remembered as a poured-out vessel, filled with the aroma of the Holy Spirit. I want to know that my life made a difference.

I walked into the conference that night where more than two thousand women had gathered to worship, hear the Word and be ministered to. I was only one of several guest speakers — certainly not the prominent one. I considered it an honor just to be there.

Taking my place on the platform, I glanced down the row at the other speakers. Hmm...beautifully coiffed hair, immaculate tailoring, shoes that actually match their outfits and handbags. Not one had a run in her panty hose. I was immediately depressed. I looked down at my outfit; it was wrinkled from traveling. The baby had missed the burp rag and puked on my shoulder. I tried to get the stain out, but it was still damp and every time I turned my head to the left I got nauseous. My stick-straight, fine hair had looked great hours earlier, but too much hair spray combined with a light rain on my run from the car to the hotel had left me looking like a drowned rat. I wanted to go home. Why couldn't I just once look like Gloria Copeland?

The praise team began to sing, "Be Glorified." As we climbed higher in worship I felt the gentle nudge of the Holy Spirit and He asked me, "Whose image do you want?"

"Lord?" I answered.

"Whose image do you want? Do you want your image or My image? Do you desire to be known as a woman of God, or do you desire to be known?" At that moment I fell on my face — right on the platform, in front of two thousand women. Weeping, repenting and worshipping my Master became my passion. I had the hands of Martha for service, but at that moment I learned what it was to have the heart of Mary.

Jesus was pleased.

2

Should I Confess It, Lay It Down, Speak It or Crucify It?

A few years ago the church went through something called the shaking. The prophets cried out that everything that can be shaken would be shaken.

God began to judge, and I'm sure many of you went through that purging. He got the ax and began sharpening it and started cutting things away. Until recently, all we could say was, "I don't know what God is doing, but I know He is doing something in me."

Unfortunately, somewhere along the way we took our faith and hope and threw it out the window. We started to believe that faith scriptures don't work. They worked in the 1970s and 80s, but they don't seem to work anymore.

But that's just not true. God's promises are as good today as they were in the 1970s or the 1500s or at any time in the short history of earth. It's time to dig up those scriptures and promises that we buried, because God will bring them to pass.

You are directly responsible for making sure that the Word of the Lord comes to pass in your life and that God doesn't bypass you. We read in Hebrews 10:35, "So do not throw away your confidence; it will be richly rewarded" (NIV).

The will of God is not based on your situation. Be aggressive in your faith to believe God, for what He told you, He will do. Proverbs 13:12 says, "Hope deferred makes the heart sick, but a desire fulfilled is a tree of life" (RSV). When hope is put off or put in the distance, what happens? You get heartsick. Is that how you're feeling now, heartsick?

For a long time, you carried a promise that you were sure was from God. You've reached a point of desperation where you now say, "I don't want to hear it anymore." Your promise has become a curse.

Let me emphasize this: God is getting ready to bring reality to those promises. The devil knows how important it is to make you sick at heart. He knows disappointment and discouragement are sure to follow.

Your hope vanishes when you experience one disappointment after another. You tell the Lord you don't think His promises will ever come to pass for you, and you begin to find your own solution to your problems.

You worry for fear you may do the wrong thing: Should I confess my problem, lay it down, speak it or crucify it? The answer is to do all these things and then stand on His Word. Confess it and take authority over the enemy of doubt and unbelief. When you come into the presence of the Father, tell Him He is more important than the promise.

First Corinthians 13:13 tells us, "And now abide faith, hope and love, these three; but the greatest of these is love" (NKJV). You know all about faith and love. You've heard it preached over and over. But I want to give you hope. I have found that you cannot have faith unless you have hope.

Delay Is Not Denial

During a meeting, the Lord gave me a word that there was a woman present with lumps in her breasts. The Lord said to me, "Tell her to come forward. Because of her sacrifice, I am going to heal and deliver her tonight." When she stepped to the front, the words of the Holy Spirit to her were, "Because of your sacrifice, I am going to show Myself and heal you."

The following night, she rushed into the meeting, eager to testify of God's goodness. "I wasn't going to go to church last night because my car broke down, but I remembered you once said that if we didn't make every effort to go to church, we may miss our miracle," she said.

"I was scheduled for surgery this morning. Since I wanted to be aware of what was happening, I asked for a local anesthetic," she continued. "The surgeon decided he needed another X-ray to make sure of where the growths were. He was called out of surgery shortly thereafter.

"Suddenly, the surgeon burst into the room, took off his mask and told me I could go home. He couldn't find any lumps in me at all."

God's promises are true. Sometimes the promises come to pass quickly, as they did for this woman. But you can't let your hope die if it doesn't happen quite so dramatically. Remember, delay is not denial!

In another meeting, the Spirit of the Lord told me to tell a woman named Kay that she should not be afraid, because the Lord had totally healed her. She would live and not die.

Now, when you speak a word like that to someone, you'd better be sure you get it right, and you'd better be sure it's God.

As I called her name, a frail little lady stood up. I delivered the word of the Lord to her. The congregation shouted and clapped as she fell under the power of the Holy Spirit.

The week before, she had been diagnosed with cancer. The doctors had said there was no hope for her. What do you think the Holy Spirit dropped into Kay's heart that night? Hope! Before she received that word, she couldn't have faith, because she didn't have any hope. The word cancer frightened her, and she had become depressed and discouraged.

That happened six years ago. I saw Kay recently in one of my meetings, and she is still rejoicing in her healing.

Many people ask me about the purpose of the prophetic word. As was evidenced in Kay's situation, I believe one of the purposes is to drop hope into your heart.

You probably know how it feels to struggle with faith when your hope has been destroyed. Your emotions start to rule you. You get a word that makes you shout and cry for a week. One week later, you need another word to keep you going.

God is getting ready to bring reality to you. Hebrews 11:1 says, "Now faith is the substance of things hoped for, the evidence of things not seen." How many times have we heard a message on this scripture, and we try with all that is within us to raise our faith just one more time? Your friends tell you to just have faith when you're going through hard times. They tell you to stop confessing your problem. You feel like hitting them with your Bible. (Of course you don't actually do it, because that's not scriptural.)

Some well-meaning Christians destroy other saints with the misuse of the Word of God, when what those hurting saints need is a pair of loving arms and an understanding heart. We want to hear that someone loves us enough to help us through our ordeal.

We read that "faith is the substance." What is substance? It is something you can put your hands on, something you can feel. Some of you miss out on faith, because you can't make faith a reality.

Romans 4:17 says, "Calls things that are not as though they were" (NIV). You can't claim something that Jesus did not promise, but you can name and claim those things that the Holy Spirit spoke into your heart. The apostle Paul tells the Ephesians that he is praying for them that God may "give unto you the spirit of wisdom and revelation...the eyes of your understanding being enlightened" (Eph. 1:17-18). Paul prayed that we would have the attainable — the spirit of revelation, which is the spirit of prophecy.

Keep the Promises Before You

I have many tape recordings of personal prophecies that were spoken to me by true prophets. I play those tapes until I can almost quote from memory what God said He was going to do for me.

God may have given you promises that you have put on the shelf. Maybe you received a prophetic word from a prophet, or maybe you heard from God directly in your own spirit. You have to restore that hope. You have to put it out in front of you. Listen to it, begin to speak it and see it come to pass. The Holy Spirit gives you hope so that you will have faith.

Paul was on a ship bound for Rome when God told him that they were going to be shipwrecked. However, no one on board heeded Paul's warnings. Before long, a violent storm struck. It raged for three days before they finally had to throw the ship's tackle overboard with their own hands (see Acts 27:19).

That's an excellent example of what happens when the enemy comes in. We are right in the middle of a storm, and we take all our promises and throw them out because our promises don't look like our circumstances. We wonder if we heard God correctly.

Part of the tackle on a boat is the compass. The crew on that ship threw overboard the very thing they needed to give them direction!

Your promise will give you direction. In the middle of the storm, you need those promises. The enemy will come in and plant doubt and unbelief. He will come in with lies to get you to throw out your promise, the very thing you need to get you through the storm.

Satan will attack you through your feelings, causing them to be hurt. He will use every weapon in his arsenal to get you to throw out the very promise of God. What the Spirit of the Lord wants you to do is to hang on to your promise.

Do you know how hope is abandoned? It's gradual. The devil knows he can't come and take your promise all at once. He waits until you get a great word from the Lord, then he slowly begins to wear away at you. He'll cause you to abandon your hope gradually.

Satan magnifies all the negatives of the situation. The crew had already decided that they were all going to die in that storm. Paul said, "Men, you should have followed my advice and not set sail from Crete and incurred this damage and loss. Let me urge you to keep up your courage."

What word can you substitute for courage? Hope!

How did Paul know that he would not die? He knew it by hope. The angel of the Lord told him that no harm would come to him, because he had an appointment to stand before Caesar. That was part of the plan. If God has put within your heart a promise, nothing can happen to you until that promise is fulfilled in your life.

Nothing stood in the way of the promise being fulfilled in Paul's life. The ship he was on ran aground and broke apart, but every life was saved. Paul was bitten by a deadly snake, but it didn't hurt him. In fact, it started a revival, as natives who witnessed this miracle accepted the truth about Jesus Christ.

For many of us, the problem is that all we know is what we

can see or comprehend. We have tunnel vision. We only see what's in front of us. Many times it's while we are dangling in the middle of a shipwreck that God gets His glory!

Don't Curse the Telephone Pole

Several years ago, I was driving what was about to become my former Toyota. As I was rounding a curve, a man suddenly appeared from nowhere and walked into the path of my car. As I swerved to miss him, the car skidded sideways toward a canal along the side of the road, wrapping itself around a telephone pole.

I flew out of my seat to the passenger side and back again. My arm was so badly cut from the glass that it required sixty-four stitches. As I was losing consciousness, I began praying in the Spirit. A paramedic thought I was delirious and speaking in a foreign language so he kept shouting at me, "In English, lady, in English!"

At the hospital, they discovered I had a broken arm, broken leg, broken collarbone and broken ribs. I had massive internal injuries and a severe concussion. I guess I was a physical mess.

My husband came as they were preparing to take me for X-rays. He said, "Stop. We'll pray first."

When my husband says "we'll pray," everyone prays whether they want to or not. He bound the spirit of death and destruction and released miracle-working power over me. After three X-rays, a technician told us there was not one broken bone.

God performed a miracle, and I was soon out of the hospital. The state trooper who first arrived on the scene came to talk to me about the accident. I told him if it hadn't been for that stupid telephone pole, I would have just hit the bank of the canal and I would have been fine. "Not so," he said. "Your car was about to flip upside down in the canal. That telephone pole saved you."

Some of us are cursing the telephone poles in our lives, not realizing that those telephone poles have been placed there by God to reveal His glory and to keep us from the enemy's true purpose.

On that ship, Paul spoke and declared what he had heard before there was any substance and before there was any evidence. And what he spoke he got, because the power of life and death is in the tongue. If we speak words of defeat instead of "God can" and "God will," we will not see the promise God has given us come to pass.

Satan will outsmart you if he can get you to start visualizing defeat and fear. Remember, hope is your springboard to faith. So many people tell you to have faith, but many of those same people have no hope.

After the birth of our first child, my husband and I desired with all our hearts to have more children. When our daughter was seven months old, we began to try to conceive another child. Several years passed, and I hadn't become pregnant.

On my daughter's fourth birthday, we asked a prophet to pray over her. He said these words, "Jerusha, like Miriam, as each new baby comes into the house, you will take care of these children for your mother and with your mother." Then he blessed her.

At the time, those words were just a nice, simple prayer. But as the years passed and I couldn't become pregnant, those words gave me hope.

I went to a fertility doctor. I took enough fertility medicine to have an entire litter, and still I couldn't become pregnant. Everyone that prayed for me got pregnant, and soon, no one would pray for me anymore.

Someone told me if my husband would wear boxer shorts, I would be able to conceive. So I stuck him in boxer shorts, but still we had no baby. Year after year went by, and as I would pass the baby furniture store along the interstate, I would tell my friends, "One day I am going to go into that store and buy a crib for my baby."

At first my friends were excited for me. But year after year passed, and they lost their hope for me. They began to console me with words like, "Cathy, be happy that you already have one child" or, "Cathy, after all, you have a wonderful ministry that God has given to you. How can you have another child and have this ministry?"

Pretty soon, when my daughter approached her sixteenth birthday and I was still declaring my hope, believing it to become substance, my friends thought I had truly gone crazy.

One day I was watching a minister on television. He said if I would just send in a vow, he would send me a prayer cloth and God would do a miracle for me. I sent in a vow and got my anointed prayer cloth, which I taped to the headboard of our bed.

My husband, who was away in Russia at the time, didn't know what I had done. Upon his return, he walked into our bedroom, looked at the prayer cloth on the headboard and said, "What in the world is that?" I said, "Never mind, baby, just get in bed and believe."

Still, there was no pregnancy and no baby, even though God did bless my vow that I had sown. Hope, coupled with the word God has spoken into your heart, will become faith, and faith will become so strong that you can smell the newborn in your arms before you ever hold it.

Some of you have been promised a mate, a man or woman of God. Your hope can be so strong you can close your eyes and smell the perfume or the aftershave of that woman or man He has promised to bring into your life. For others of you, you can see yourself sitting behind a desk that God has promised will be yours upon the promotion in your job.

Enter the Field of Hope

Ruth was one woman who had good reason to lose hope.

Her husband had died, famine was in the land, and all she had left was her mother-in-law, Naomi.

> And Naomi said, Turn again, my daughters: why will ye go with me? are there yet any more sons in my womb, that they may be your husbands? (Ruth 1:11).

But Ruth's hope was strong, even though she had lost everything. She had lost her husband. She was childless. Yet, she saw something in Naomi that made her want to follow her and be a part of her life. She claimed Naomi's God as her God. But Naomi said to her, "I have no hope. Maybe God has turned His back on me" (see v. 12).

Many times when we are waiting for the promise to come to pass, it seems as though God has truly turned His back on us. I can see Ruth and Naomi walking back to the land together, leaving Moab. Ruth was excited and asked Naomi, "Tell me what it's like. What can we expect? I know God, your God, is going to do something for us!"

Hope is contagious. Being around people with hope is exciting. Hope is the realm that overcomes the realm of the natural. That's why you can get healed. This is the realm where miracles come from.

Naomi realized she had a determined woman on her hands, and all of a sudden Naomi's hope was activated. "You know, Ruth, I do have a relative named Boaz." Ruth had hope. She got out of the house, got to work, got noticed and got blessed.

> And, behold, Boaz came from Bethlehem, and said unto the reapers, The Lord be with you. And they answered him, The Lord bless thee. Then said Boaz unto his servant that was set over the reapers, Whose damsel is this? (Ruth 2:4-5).

Boaz couldn't even respond properly to their greeting. His servants said, "How are you?" And he said, "Yes, how are you? And who's the young babe in the field?" Ruth didn't sit around twiddling her thumbs; she had a hope that got her up and moving. Finally, in Ruth 2:8 her hope takes on substance — in the form of Boaz.

Hope is not idle. Hope will make you active. If you are going to receive from God, you have to have a hope that is so real you can smell the victory. You know the job is going to come. The answer is going to come. The healing is going to come because you are already in the field.

How long does it take? What does it matter how long it takes? If you will get in the field, God will give you the answer. If Satan can get you hopeless and get you to stay out of the field, you will have nothing.

You need to stir up your hope realm. There's even a word for the place where young girls store a bunch of melamine dishes that they will use to serve a burned hot dog and some macaroni and cheese to their newlywed husband some day. It's called a hope chest. If you're ever going to have what you desire, you must stop talking the negative and enter into the hope realm.

Hope is your springboard to faith. Faith will bring substance and evidence. That will be your miracle.

I refused to give up my hope of holding my newborn baby. In the last two years the Lord has put four of them into my arms. However, turning my hope into faith and substance proved almost more than I could bear.

I was thrilled beyond belief to hear the adoption agency had a baby for us. All the details were worked out, and in six months we would finally become parents again. Finally — the promise was coming to pass.

They called us the day the baby boy (whom we named Gabriel Levi) was born. "I'm sorry Cathy. The birth mother changed her mind. She's keeping the baby."

We wept. I raged, "God, how could You allow this. It's not fair! How cruel to finally get my hopes up and for what?"

Our congregation stood along with us in this valley as we called our son into our home. Gathering ourselves, my husband and I held hands declaring, "God, You are not cruel. You are not a liar. You are a faithful God who can be trusted. You love us, You love Gabriel and You love his birth mother. We surrender our son to Your perfect will, but we will never surrender our hope or our promise to the enemy!"

Almost two years later, I was sitting in a chair in my bedroom reading when my daughter raced through the door. The adoption agency called to tell me Gabriel's mother was going to sign the papers. She couldn't cope any longer. Bursting into tears I heard the Lord speak, "The son that the enemy stole from you, I'm giving back into your arms."

I called my husband, who was ministering in Korea at the time and told him what had happened. I asked him what he sensed the Lord saying, and he confirmed what the Lord had spoken to me. "Honey," he said, "the Lord told me that the son the enemy took from us is being restored."

That night I went to bring our son home. Reaching into the back seat to pick up the sleeping toddler, I began to bless the Lord. Waking up, Gabriel looked at me and said, "Momma, Momma," as he put his little head back on my shoulder and went back to sleep.

It took two years, but God had brought our son home.

Don't give up your hope! Your promise is just around the corner. Remember, the harvest is one step beyond the faint!

3

More Manure, Please

It was a difficult Christmas season for us. Our twenty-month-old adopted daughter, Hannah, was suffering from a rare blood disorder that is almost always fatal. Doctors first thought she had scarlet fever. However, her symptoms worsened and she stopped eating and drinking. Her joints became terribly swollen in a matter of weeks and soon she couldn't walk. A specialist finally diagnosed her as having Kawasaki, a disease that is most common in young Japanese children.

For the two weeks before Christmas, we had taken turns

holding her and gently massaging her joints. Our intercessory prayer partners stood with us in believing God for a miracle.

Seated around the dining room table, we attempted to enjoy our Christmas dinner. After we blessed the food, Hannah made a circle with her arms and said, "God loves the whole wide world!" We all wept as she said it over and over. God used her to testify of His love on His Son's birthday! From that moment on, she slowly began to heal.

Is it possible to have peace despite the pressures of life — the healings, the promotions, the deep desires that just don't come according to our timetable? We start a new year believing we are going to see the promises of God come to pass this year. Then we realize, "I believed that last year." But the Word of God tells us to hope to the end, despite what we see — or don't see — on the outside.

Paul says, "So, I say, live by the Spirit, and you will not gratify the desires of the sinful nature" (Gal. 5:16, NIV). Further on he tells us the acts of the sinful nature include: sexual immorality, impurity and debauchery, idolatry and witchcraft, hatred, discord, jealousy, fits of rage, selfish ambition, dissension, factions and envy, drunkenness, orgies and the like.

We read further that the fruit of the Spirit takes on these characteristics: love, joy, peace, patience, kindness, goodness, faithfulness, gentleness and self-control.

You may think, "But sexual immorality, drunkenness and jealousy aren't *my* problems." The problems you do have, though, are those that will still keep you from inheriting the promise of God. Maybe you've never had an illicit encounter in a motel room, but you do struggle with depression and discouragement. Perhaps, like me, you struggle with patience. It doesn't matter; they're all enemies of peace.

Many Christians are highly developed in their gifts but are lacking development in their character. Even baby believers are able to prophesy accurately, though their character is undeveloped. But the apostle Paul says, "I don't care if you prophesy and you speak mysteries to men and presidents, and yet if you don't have love, you have not character to go along with your gift. You are as a 'sounding brass and a tinkling cymbal' " (see 1 Cor. 13:1).

The fact that a person is in ministry is no indication that he or she has developed the fruit of the Spirit. I know of some who have been in the ministry for years, yet they don't possess love, joy, peace, patience, kindness, goodness, faithfulness, gentleness and self-control. They are always frustrated, worried, fearful and anxious. They can tell you all about the great miracles God has done through them, but their character stinks.

A lady once prayed this way for me: "Lord, I thank You she's going to have a more accurate word. You're going to take her deeper." I thought to myself, "I bind that. I don't want it. I've just arrived to where I am and I want to stay here for a while and enjoy the fruit before I go on to a new level. I know that new levels bring new devils, and I'm comfortable right here for now."

Everyone struggles with the devil. The more ministry you're engaged in, the bigger the battle. Your character will determine how you handle those battles. There's only one way you can measure yourself in the fruit of character, and that's by your reactions. How do you behave at home? How do you act in pressure situations?

We have a lovely gas fireplace in our bedroom which we admire often and dust occasionally. One cool evening, as we were lying in bed, we decided it would be nice to have a fire. Understand that we didn't have a clue as to how to light the thing. We finally succeeded in turning it on but didn't know if the doors should be opened or shut.

You've heard it said that when all else fails, read the instructions. In doing so, about two hours later, we discovered the manual warned that you must have ventilation in the room or you may not wake up. We jumped up and opened the door.

Then we were freezing. It occurred to me that I would either come down with pneumonia or not wake up at all. I turned to my husband and jokingly said, "Just when we're coming out of the valley, when we've withstood the pressure the devil has put on us, you're going to kill me."

How do you respond in pressure situations? Do you say, "I don't know what happened to me. I just lost it. This is really not the real me." Oh, yes it is. When you put your thumb in a soda bottle and shake it, what is going to come out when you remove your thumb? Soda, of course. Remember, whatever is in you when you are stepped on is going to come squishing out!

Who Are You Trying to Impress?

My pastor's wife told me she was worshipping the Lord one morning, weeping in His presence. The Lord said to her, "Your ministry doesn't impress me. Your teaching doesn't impress me."

She thought, "Just when you and I were having such a wonderful time together."

He further said, "Your ministry and teaching don't impress Me because it all comes from Me. Do you know what impresses Me? It is your personal dedication."

What impresses God is our personal dedication to Him. It's how we choose to respond in the middle of difficult situations. Do we respond with fear or with faith?

A woman used to come to me before every meeting, the minute I entered the door. She managed to dump on me just as I was about to minister. She just had to have a word from the Lord — again. What she really wanted was for me to tell her that everything was going to be OK and that she would never have any more problems.

Finally, after weeks of this, I took her by the shoulders and asked her not to fill my mind with garbage as I was about to minister. I told her I hurt for her, loved her and wished I could take away all her suffering.

I wasn't minimizing her problems, but this is not how to get a word from God. There are some things you simply must go through yourself. The beautiful truth is that God will walk through it with you

Hang in There!

Longsuffering is simply hanging in there for as long as it takes. You aren't born with this quality — it must be developed. How do we develop it? Through pressure!

Recently, my husband and I were going through a financial crisis. In the past, through times like this, we've discovered that God was using these crises to bring us closer to Himself. He was using the pressure to cause us to grow in faith and dependence on Him.

Pressure is an often-repeated theme in the Bible. Look at the three Hebrew men who were thrown into the furnace — that's pressure. Our first reaction would no doubt be to look for a way out; consequently, we would not grow in our faith. When the king looked into the furnace, he saw not three but four men in there — and not one of them burned by the flames (see Daniel 3). That's growth under pressure. That is what God wants.

A good teacher will always give you an out. I homeschool my daughter, and when I am ready to give her a test, I always go over the material again and again. If I see she is not grasping the material well enough to pass the test, I give her a few more days for review.

God is the Master Teacher. He loves us so much that He gives us one opportunity after another to change the condition we're in. He is like a good teacher who says, "We'll just go around the mountain again until you pass the test."

One day I was complaining to my pastor, "I love my children.

I would never allow awful things to happen to them. Why is God allowing all these problems to come into my life? I am a giver, above and beyond my tithes."

He looked at me. "And so we accuse the Most High God," he said. Squish! I was stepped on and I didn't like what was coming out. I didn't even know that yucky stuff was in there.

Don't look for a way out. Stay in the middle of the pressure situation. Pressure is what causes the coal to become a diamond. Life is a test, and the way you overcome situations determines your position.

Marriage, Divorce or Murder?

My husband and I have been through some hard times during our marriage. There were times when I wished that God would just take him, because I was going to divorce him if God didn't kill him first. I know Randi felt the same way about me at times.

Does that shock you? There were times I wanted to leave, times I could have left. There were times I prayed my car would slam into a telephone pole and I would be killed, because I felt death was the only way out of my suffering. At times when Randi hurt me the most, I asked God for permission to divorce him. And there were times when I hurt him so badly that he didn't want to be married to me any longer.

We learned a valuable lesson in those pressure situations: We had better come through this together, because so many people were watching how we handled the pressure. Many lay people have the privilege of living in brick houses. But those in ministry live in glass houses. We are constantly being watched in pressure situations.

The Lord told me, "If you want to go, you can. I'll still bless you. But if you'll stay, I'll anoint you and increase you and cause My grace to be on your life. I'll give you a brand new heart. I'll rekindle the love you had for your husband and the love your husband had for you if you'll stay in this situation."

It was a very unlovely situation, and I didn't want to stay. But we decided we had to hold on to each other and say, "Bless God, we are going to go through this together. If we don't, how are the weaker couples going to make it? We can't show others how to do this if we can't do it ourselves."

Patience is going through afflictions, pain, toil, calamity, provocation or other evil with a calm, unruffled temper.

When you desperately need a word from God, it's often not faith you lack but patience.

No one can take you to the place where you acquire patience; you have to go there yourself. And you get there by enduring what you are going through without murmuring and complaining. Endurance is the act of waiting long for justice.

How can you develop this fruit? You'll never develop it in a calm environment. You have to develop it in an environment that demands the opposite reaction. Your flesh wants to panic. But if you can endure under pressure, you will develop patience.

The Secret Is Manure

I'm not very good with plants. I was once given an ivy; it's still living and I can't understand why. I always forget to water it, and then I overcompensate by pouring a gallon of water on it. I'm sure it's a hard-to-kill variety. I prefer silk arrangements. All you have to do is dust them.

What is it that makes the prettiest tree with the sweetest fruit? What is one of the main factors that causes the plant to thrive? Manure! You know what the manure of life is: when you go to bed and everything is great, only you wake up in the morning to find someone has pooped all over your front yard. Then you get an overdraft notice in the mail, and everything goes from bad to worse.

Real love can grow, even flourish, when you are in a pressure situation. You may experience depression, worry, fear, and the need to blame someone. That's an environment where real love can grow. That's when the real fruit of the Spirit will prosper in your life, when the pressure is on.

The world loses itself searching for peace with drugs, alcohol or hours of mind-numbing "entertainment" on television. But no matter what kind of situation you are in, you can find peace. Jesus said, "Peace I leave with you; my peace I give you. I do not give to you as the world gives" (John 14:27, NIV).

You can walk in peace in the middle of your pressure situation. You can have it without a prophetic word from me. You can have perfect peace by making a decision and saying, "I will be a vessel of honor in the middle of this pressure, because I *choose* to be."

I was given two beautiful rosebushes by a friend. All spring, I watered and weeded my prize rosebushes which grew to an enormous three feet tall!

One day my grandmother (affectionately known as "Gammy") was visiting me, and I took her by the hand to proudly display my rosebushes.

I boasted, "Look how green, how tall. Can you believe it Gammy. I can never grow anything and yet — behold!"

"They don't have any roses on them," she said matter-of-factly.

"Yes, but see how large and alive they are," I added slightly irritated.

"They don't have any roses on them," she repeated.

By this time, I'm beginning to think, Lord, she's had a good eighty-eight years — take her home. The nerve of her not appreciating my gift of horticulture. With that my dear, precious grandmother walked into the garage and emerged with an enormous pair of hedge clippers. To my utter horror, she whacked off three-fourths of my prized rose limbs.

"There" she said triumphantly, handing me the apparatus of death. "Water and fertilize them." Two weeks later to my amazement the bushes were covered with beautiful, plentiful rosebuds! Now with every cut of the gardener's tool, I can feel the hand of the husbandman on me.

I know sometimes doing the will of God seems intolerable. Many problems appear to have no known end in sight. Our Lord desires not only fruit, but rather more fruit. We can be tall, gangling and thorny, but the Lord says, "There's no fruit." In His love for us, He prunes, fertilizes and waters our lives. Don't resist the pruning of the Lord; this is the very thing that will cause the fruit to abound.

4

Sometimes That's Life!

When I was growing up, the whole object of salvation was to get to heaven when you die. Just hang in there until it was your time to go. That was the message of the day.

Then I married Randi, a crazy Jewish man with no religious background or training who said to me, "We can have fun now. We can serve God and still enjoy the blessings of the Lord now."

The Word says the kingdom of God is righteousness, peace, and joy in the Holy Spirit. But how are you going to get these things? You may have to go through many trials to get to that place.

There are many Christians who don't want to pay the price. They don't want to go through trials. I include myself in this category. I'd rather go on vacation, but we all have our tribulations. We are living in a time when it seems the devil is bringing a greater destructive force against Christians. He is magnifying his efforts against us, our children and our ministries.

Because of this, we need one another. The very one you despise may be the one the Lord will use to encourage you. Christians who are stressed out and weary in their tribulations give up. They surrender to their emotions, which results in a life with no victory. You need to say, "With God's help, I'll never give up."

Look What God Provided for Dinner

You've probably seen the movie *Jurassic Park,* in which a massive experiment involving dinosaurs went awry. These enormous dinosaurs that had been created for pleasure started to chase the people and eat them. The people panicked.

That is the way some Christians are when a trial comes into their lives. They throw up their hands and say, "Dear God, what are we going to do? It's a trial." But the child of God who understands this truth does not look at the size of the dinosaur, but says, "Look what God has provided for dinner."

Some of you are running from your dinosaurs instead of saying, "Look what God has entrusted to me."

I would love to believe that it is God's perfect will to pluck us up out of the hard places and plant us beside still water, but I know it doesn't work that way. We have to go through the hardships, and we have to overcome pressures in the mind as well as in the body.

Our Abagael is just a little baby. Her cradle is beside my

bed, so when she cries at night, I get up and change her diaper and feed her. I will hold her until she gets past her crisis. I find the cause of her discomfort, fix it and then rock her until she goes back to sleep.

Hannah, who is two, can crawl out of her crib. After we put her to bed, she invariably will come out of her room and tell us she doesn't want to go to bed. We march her right back into her room and firmly put her back to bed, and she knows better than to get up again.

Samuel and Gabriel are at a stage in their lives where they are entertained by sitting in their high chairs with a tray full of little turkey sticks that they can eat as they mash them and spread them all through their hair.

When my eighteen-year-old daughter, Jerusha, tells me, "I'm hungry," I tell her she knows where the refrigerator is. It has sandwich stuff in it, and she can fix herself something to eat.

That's the way it is in the kingdom of God as we mature in the Lord. We want Him to coddle us, but He tells us, "You know where the refrigerator is, where the storehouse of promises and blessings are. I know there's a dinosaur coming at you, but he's your dinner. Go get him."

If you apply these principles to your life, you'll walk with stability and in victory. That doesn't mean that there won't be any more trials, and it doesn't mean that you are to avoid or run away from the problems. It means that when they do come, they won't knock you off your feet or persuade you to call a thousand intercessors to pray for you.

As a Christian walking through these hard places, you can rise above them and say, "God, I thank You for this opportunity that You have given to me." You can't do it alone. He promises never to leave us or forsake us. As baby Christians we needed coddling, holding, reassuring. We will continue to need some of that; however, as we mature in the Lord, He teaches us how to stand when the going gets rough.

There are some who try to avoid the problem and say, "I'll

just trust God." You can't avoid it. You must have active faith. The children of Israel said, "We want out. We don't want to go through this wilderness or face giants. We don't want trials, we just want manna." They got to wander around for forty years before going into the promised land.

Many Christians fall apart when things aren't going the way they want them to. You can know that God is with you, and He'll bring you through as gold refined seven times in the fire.

God will delay the test, but I'd rather learn as quickly as possible so I can go on. Sometimes delaying the test prolongs the suffering.

Everything is not necessarily the direct result of a test or temptation from the devil. Sometimes it's just plain life. If you deal with it the way God wants you to, you'll grow in the Lord; you'll be stronger in the things of God, and you will receive deliverance.

Recently, I was the speaker at a conference where nothing seemed to be going smoothly. My mother, Rose, who often travels with me, was there and sensed this. She asked me if I was frustrated. My answer was, "No, I have already dealt with this problem before I ever got here. We're just going to flow with them, and we are going to be servants. We will yield ourselves and put a love on these ladies and watch God do miracles. Let everyone else run around and be upset."

I told her we were going to respond with dignity and grace. We were going to honor the Lord in the midst of this confusion, and God was going to deliver us. And He did! We had a wonderful conference.

You have to flow in the Spirit when everything and everyone is going in different directions.

Trials Do Have a Purpose

There are two purposes for trials in our lives. God has a purpose, and so does Satan.

47

We know that Satan's purpose is to steal, kill, destroy and instill fear in you. He wants you to run, and he would like for you to give up, doubt, cave in and lose your faith in God. He plants doubt as to what God has spoken into your life. You received a promise, or a prophetic word, but the circumstances in your life are the opposite of what God's prophecy was to you.

Abraham received a promise from God: His seed would bless the whole world. But the circumstance was that Sarah was barren and stayed that way until long after her child-bearing years. However, that circumstance did not nullify God's promise.

If you stop being aggressive against the enemy, you'll miss your destiny in life. The Lord will say to you, "You made it in, but you never fulfilled the destiny I had for you, because of your self-pity. You never really got hold of My promise to you. Instead, you let doubt come in; therefore, you missed the best I had for you."

The Word tells us to resist the devil. The word *resist* means to oppose. We oppose the devil by not throwing away our trust, our faith and our confidence in God.

Mind Your Mind

There are places where I won't let my mind travel because the enemy attacks us in our thoughts.

We rehearse gossip without realizing the importance of disciplining our minds not to go into those areas. Also, we know the devil would like for us to dwell on things from the past, such as old wounds and old hurts. He wants us to push the rewind button on things that bring pain to us, and he tries to bring accusations against our brothers and sisters in the Lord.

The minute I sense that happening in my mind, I talk to Satan and say, "I'm not going to go into that area, Devil. You lose." I recapture my thoughts and bring my mind back to the things of God, His Word and His promises.

The enemy wants you to fall on your face in the midst of your tribulation and cry, "Why, God, why?" Our Father speaks to us and says, "My grace is sufficient for you."

There are many Christians who are shipwrecked in their faith because they did not understand why God did not answer in the time and in the way they expected. Consequently, they surrendered the promise and gave in to discouragement. Complete and total trust in God is the means you must use to overcome discouragement and to receive His promise.

Job said, "Though he slay me, yet will I hope in him" (Job 13:15, NIV). It wasn't God who was killing Job. He wasn't trying to kill him at all, and God isn't trying to slay you either! He wants good things for you more than you want them for yourself.

You can say with victory, "The situation on my job, in my family or my church may not be as I would like it to be right now, but I am not going to back away from what You promised. You gave me a promise, and I'm going to walk through this situation without whining and complaining but with dignity, even though I don't understand everything."

I Speak From Experience

I once wanted to give up on everything at a hard time in my life. I went to my meetings and did all the things I was expected to do, but no one knew what I was going through in my own life, in my personal walk. No one could imagine the suffering, pain and heartache I was experiencing.

It was only the grace of God that brought me through. It was not Cathy Lechner, because she would have checked out and run as far away as she could.

Month after month, as I went through the motions, the Lord would speak to me and say, "Get up and go because My grace is sufficient for you. You can go on because I am going to help you." I would say, "I don't have anything to give to anyone because I need something myself. I have no hope for myself. How can I give hope to anyone else?"

Again the Lord spoke to me: "Just persevere." I knew if I didn't keep going, if I gave in to despair, the devil would use my defeat to defeat others.

I began to do battle against the devil. I wanted all who were watching me to know that I would overcome. They could say, "She isn't going to die through this pain. She is going to make it!"

People will follow in your footsteps, and if you give up, you will affect them as well as your household. Satan will try to destroy your influence by robbing you of your faith and victory.

If you will war against the enemy and get into the Word of God, victory will come. It will rub off on those around you and give them hope and bring deliverance. God wants to encourage you and let you know of His love for you. He will minister and speak into your life.

> I have great confidence in you; I take great pride in
> you. I am greatly encouraged; in all *our* troubles my
> joy knows no bounds (2 Cor. 7:4, NIV, italics added).

Our perspective is usually different from Paul's. We say, "In all *my* trials, I can't wait to get out. In all *my* trials, I can't wait to get to a meeting to get a word to find out when it's going to end."

When I am going through a hard place, I would like for my husband to say to me, "Baby, I'm so sorry you are going through this. Here, take this charge card and go get yourself a little something to cheer you up."

Sorry, it doesn't work that way in my house. He says, "You are worrying about this situation, and what good is it doing?" I know he is right, but I still want to be comforted and pitied.

I also know that he could hold me all day, but in the end, it won't change the situation.

God says, "I want you to rise up and begin to declare that you are going to make it through."

Nehemiah, in the worst of circumstances said, "Eat the fat, and drink the sweet, and send portions unto them for whom nothing is prepared...for the joy of the Lord is your strength" (Neh. 8:10).

"Eating and drinking the sweet" sounds like a party to me, with cake and ice cream. Have a party in the midst of your trials. Let your joy know no bounds. Go through your trials with dignity. God is not out to get you. He's out to get you through.

5

You Learn Contentment by Not Having What You Want

If you want to get rich quick, move to Hollywood and become a plastic surgeon. People, with all their wealth and fame, are continually trying to suck it out here and put it in there. I confess: I always wanted to look like a combination of Princess Di and Loni Anderson. But it's just not going to happen, because I have a short Italian mother and I know I'm never going to be 5'11". I am going to be 5'2" forever. What's worse, I've heard your body shrinks as you get older.

What is obvious is that people are just not content. Some are not happy with who they are or where they live. Others are not happy with their height or their weight. You buy a new car, and the next newer model is loaded with more bells and whistles, making yours outdated. How about that computer you just bought? Can it talk to you? The new ones can.

Many Christians can't even rejoice in prayers that have been answered, because there are always other unanswered prayers. They live in a place where they cannot be content with who they are or how their lives are going.

It's the plan of the enemy to make you discontented with life. He wants you discontented with your church, your pastor, your singlehood.

Are you discontented with your spouse? I often hear comments like, "I'm married, but I don't like my husband. I wish he could be different. I wanted a combination of an astronaut, neurosurgeon, attorney, Kenneth Copeland-type. How did I get *him?*"

The Lord spoke this to me: "Daughter, all the devil has to do to get you frustrated or discontented is to shift your focus from what you have to what you do not have."

Lucifer was the father of frustration. He wasn't happy being the chief choirmaster in heaven and leading the masses in worshipping God. He rose up and said, "I want to be like the Most High God." He wasn't even contented with that desire. He began to sow seeds of discontentment into mankind. He said to Eve, "Yes, you have the whole garden, but what about those two trees over there?" Satan's ploy is discontentment.

Philippians 4:4 says, "Rejoice in the Lord always. I will say it again: Rejoice!" (NIV). Now, you can't rejoice unless you first 'joice!'

Are you discouraged and downhearted? At the risk of sounding gross, you can't regurgitate until you have first eaten something. So I repeat, you can't rejoice until you have first 'joiced.'

That's what praise and worship is about. When we praise and worship we are trying to break free of the bond of discon-

tentment. But *you* have to be the one to do it. *You* press in and
worship the Lord.

Some of you say, "I just can't." One of the hardest things to
get people to do is to break through into praise. They say,
"It's not my personality. I don't want to. All I want is a
word." And God tells you, "You've already had twenty-five
words...break free! I'll say it again, rejoice!"

We charismatics love the verse that says, "I can do everything through him who gives me strength" (Phil. 4:13, NIV).
But we don't read it in the context in which Paul was writing.
Paul said it's work. He said you need to pray, give thanks,
think about the right things and practice what you've learned
(vv. 6,8-9).

Paul admits he wasn't born content; no one laid hands on
him to make him content. He worked at it. Achieving contentment is a learning process. My favorite definition of
contentment is living independent of the circumstances. I have
learned this way of living. No matter what is going on around
me, I have learned to be content. If you want to be successful
in God, be willing to go through this learning process.

Serving With an Attitude

God has been speaking this into my life: "If you want to be
a giant in the kingdom of God, just do what 98 percent of the
body of Christ does not do...read, pray, give and be thankful."
Whether I drive a pickup or I get picked up in a limousine, it is
my thankful attitude that makes the difference.

Have you ever cried and said, "I don't know why God isn't
working for me"? God is working for you. He is changing circumstances. He does love you. You do have promises. It's
your attitude while you are driving that pickup, in that hard
place, living in a house with no air conditioning or while you
are at that job you don't like, that counts. It's your attitude
while you are in those circumstances that determines whether

you will be able to go on to the next place God has for you.

For a while, we were without a salary because of a church split, and both of our cars were repossessed. It's hard to have a traveling ministry without a car. So someone arranged for us to rent one. We rented this horrible, horrible car. It seemed like a 1901 model to me. I can't recall what it was except it was horrible. It was big, it was loud, and it was horrible. I hated the thing.

My daughter Jerusha and I nicknamed this horrible car "Jaws" because it was gray (like a shark) and ate gas like crazy. It would go chug-a-lugging down the road, and inevitably it would break down in the middle of an intersection. Jerusha, who was just a little girl at the time, would say, "I'm not getting in that car anymore, Mommy. I'm ashamed because it always breaks down, and we have to push it across the main road."

I was murmuring and complaining to the Lord. Finally, the Lord convicted me and showed me that I was not grateful. I told Him I was paying $175 a month rent on this old car. He said, "I am providing for you." So I took Jaws out and gave her a shampoo and set. I swept out all those stale french fries — you know, the kind that always manage to find a place under the seat, especially if you have children. I sucked out all the junk and cleaned that puppy up. I polished it and started blessing that car and thanking the Lord for it, knowing that I wasn't going to have to drive it much longer. God had something better for me. I was determined not to murmur and grumble and complain about it.

It was about a month or two later when God moved in our behalf and upgraded us to a better car. The lesson? I had to learn contentment.

Know Who You Are in God

The United States is the richest country in the world. For most Americans, all our needs are met. We don't think they are, but we have health plans, dental plans, food stamps for the poor and much more. We don't know what it is to have war in our country. I know we have a great deal of violence, but would you like to move to Bosnia, Cuba or Rwanda? There are a lot of vacancies in those countries.

Even though we are a blessed nation, more people die from suicide than murder in the United States. We always hear about the large number of murders and not about suicide statistics, though the suicide rate is higher. Why are so many committing suicide? Because there is something wrong inside. The whole premise of advertising is to make us discontented. The TV ads tell us we can have it all and have it our way. We want to reach the highest heights, drive the best car and live in an elite neighborhood. Image is everything. It doesn't matter if an outfit looks disgusting as long as the label is right.

I was in an airport waiting for a plane when some teenage guys came strutting by, really trying to look cool. Of course, they all wanted to look like they were different from each other, but they were all stamped out of the same mold.

They had on shorts. Well, not really shorts...they were kind of short-longs. The crotch was dragging on the floor, and their underwear was hanging out of the top.

As I watched them, I thought, "How many people did they buy these shorts for?" I wanted to run over and pull them up. Three people could fit into one pair of them. Their shoes were too big and unlaced. They had names cut into their hair, and they really thought they were cool. I was laughing at them to myself when I heard the Spirit caution me, "Cathy, it isn't nice to laugh at people." I repented, but I was sure I heard the Lord say, "I thought it was funny, too."

People want to look like everyone else. If you are secure in yourself, you don't have to look like everyone around you. You know who you are in God. If you are in ministry, your ministry doesn't have to look like everyone else's. If your ministry is different from everyone else's, don't get puffed up and think yours is better either. Stay humble. Stay small before God. We are just little ants that God could step on if He so chose.

Our Second Nature

What is the last thing you complained about? Have you complained about your lively kids? Would you rather have them in a wheelchair? Do you complain about your husband? Tell yourself, "I married the right person." That settles it once and for all.

During my appearance on a TV show, the producer mistakenly displayed my home address on the screen instead of the studio's. Now I have a stack of letters from single women in that area who want a word from God. Do you know what they all want, without exception? A husband!

I suggested to my secretary that if we could send these discontented, single women some of the difficult spouses we know for a few days, we'd see how long they would be content with a husband. The enemy will do whatever he can to make you discontent.

I was talking to a pastor who was angry and upset with his church. He said, "This is such a small congregation. I deserve better than this." I told him he wasn't going anywhere, because his attitude stunk. I have found that we have what God can trust us with.

Discontentment can be stirred up by other people. Don't let negative people dump on you. Don't hang around gossipers. For every one minute of negative you listen to, it takes six minutes of positive to shift back. Refuse to listen. Quote the scripture, "Whatsoever things are of good report...think on these things" (Phil. 4:8). Negative people have the problem. Pray for them.

The Word says the person who takes up the offense of another is blocked from the presence of God (see Mark 11:25).

It also says that God inhabits the praise of His people (see Psalm 22:3). Guess whose spirit inhabits the gossipers, the grumblers?

On the way to a meeting in Philadelphia, God began to deal with me about complaining and grumbling. While my mother and I waited for our flight at the Jacksonville airport, I said to her, "I really want you to help me. I don't want to murmur or complain, and I don't want to grumble. I want you to help me by reminding me every time I do it."

She asked me if I was going to get mad at her when she did, and I assured her I wouldn't. Shortly after our conversation, the announcement came over the intercom that our flight to Philadelphia was going to be delayed due to plane trouble. You know, the usual: The wing fell off and as soon as we get some duct tape, some masking tape or some super glue we'll get that thing stuck back on, and we'll load you all on, and we'll take off.

I thought, "Great, this is going to make us late." My mind was racing ahead to the rental car that was supposed to be waiting for us.

We ended up flying first class at no extra charge. I love first class, because instead of throwing the peanuts at you, the flight attendants gently lay them on the tray in front of you.

As we were getting comfortably settled in our seats, a child sat in front of us. This same child always sits near me; she follows me everywhere. She turned around and said, "Hey, hey." After a while came, "Hey, I dropped my game. Hey, hey." I said, "Turn around, sweetheart, and sit down or you're going to fall out of the plane." Even my mom was getting perturbed at her performance.

Finally, I said, "Sit down right now, honey, or I'm going to punch your eyes out." I love children. I just have a problem with the parents who won't control them.

We arrived at the airport and hurried to the car rental office where my husband had reserved a large-sized car for me. He likes me to have one of those when I'm on a strange highway and don't know where I am going, which happens often.

I showed the rental agent the papers and told him I was there to pick up my car. He told me they didn't even have that model car. I insisted that I wanted a large car, any model. Same answer. He assured us that we could have the best car on the lot and presented us with this little clown car. I think the name of the agency was We Make It, You Skate It.

He told me it was the best car in the whole world. God drives this car. He was highly insulted when I pointed out that our luggage wouldn't even fit in it. To top it off, the instructions were in Arabic. The horn was falling out over the steering wheel, the mirror was dangling and somehow I had managed to turn on the wipers but didn't have a clue as how to turn them off. I just knew this was a plot of the devil to destroy me.

It was getting late so we crammed ourselves and our luggage in our little car and were told to take Interstate 95 north for a thirty-minute ride to our hotel in Philadelphia. After driving about an hour, we began to get suspicious, especially when my mom asked me if we were supposed to see a "Welcome to New Jersey" sign. I told her that her eyes were failing her in her maturity, but I had to repent when I saw a sign that read, "New Jersey Turnpike, next exit."

Thank God for car phones. At midnight, I called the pastor who was hosting the conference and told him we were lost. You can imagine our surprise when we learned that we were supposed to be on Interstate 95 south. We were given incorrect directions, which meant we had to go all the way back and start over.

As I sat with my knees under my chin and my suitcase hitting me in the head every time the car hit a bump, I began to fume. I couldn't believe this! I'm five hours late already, I have to minister to all those people, and those crazy people at the car rental agency messed me up...and on and on. My mom sat and listened for a while. Then she said those words I did not want to hear, "Now, when do you want this complaining thing to start?"

I slowed down and told her to get out of the car. She could sell her tapes and sing her way home. But I was sure I could hear the Holy Spirit say, "Gotcha!"

It's second nature for us to complain about everything. Complain in the restaurant, complain to the waitress, complain about the church service, complain about everything.

Do You Want to Serve Your Enemies?

There's a verse that helps me stop complaining. It's Deuteronomy 28:47.

> Because you did not serve the Lord your God with joy and gladness of heart, for the abundance of everything, therefore you shall serve your enemies, whom the Lord will send against you, in hunger, in thirst, in nakedness, and in need of everything; and He will put a yolk of iron on your neck until He has destroyed you (NKJV).

That's why there are so many people who want things from God and see nothing coming to pass. They have not served the Lord their God with joy and gladness for the abundance of all things. They have served their enemies instead. What are the enemies? Sickness, poverty, continual lack, grief, brokenness, loneliness, sorrow, depression, fear, anxiety and frustration.

God said, "Because you didn't serve Me with gladness of heart, you may be like the children of Israel, always wondering why you never come into the promised land." God desires for us to learn from those enemies. He wants us to practice serving Him with joy and gladness in the circumstances He has provided right now.

God has really nailed me to the wall at times about my

complaints. On one occasion, we had just cleaned the kitchen in preparation for the celebration of Samuel's first birthday. Samuel and Hannah had their baths and were in their pajamas. All we had to do was to eat some cake, get a few pictures and then send them off to bed, right? Wrong!

Samuel had already done the traditional thing...you know, grab the middle of the cake and squish it in his fingers. I thought, "A little wash rag will do the job." About that time Hannah decided she wanted to get into the act. So she crawled up behind Samuel's booster chair, grabbed a handful of cake, icing and all, rubbed her hands together and proceeded to smear it all through his hair.

The whole place was a disaster area. My first reaction was to scream, "I just bathed you! I just cleaned the floor!" But somehow the words stuck in my throat. For years I longed to have babies sitting at my table, smearing cake all over the place. So my scream changed to, "Thank You, Lord. It's just crumbs. The kids will wash." God made them that way — wash and wear.

We immediately tend to focus on the negative. We focus on how much more work it's going to be and how hard it is. It seems that we never get to park in front of the church, we never get to sit in "our" pew and we complain so much we can't serve the Lord with joy in abundance. Remember He said, "If you don't serve Me, I will let you serve your enemies."

If you are not looking at your situation right now and saying, "I am going to serve the Lord with joy and gladness of heart," then you are serving your enemies. When people ask how you are, try answering, "I'm blessed." Does it mean you are not struggling? No. But your answer can still be, "I'm blessed." Be thrilled with what Jesus has done in your life.

Bible translator Ben Campbell Johnson paraphrases Philippians 4:12-13 this way:

I can accept put-downs or recognition, in fact I have

become adept at all kinds of existence. I can go hungry or I can go full, I can handle wealth or I can have little. I have learned to do all things with a right attitude because Christ is the energizing center of my life.

Can you say this? "He is my center, He is my all in all. It doesn't matter what happens. It doesn't matter how the enemy tries to shake, rattle, rock and roll my cage. It doesn't matter if things don't come to pass the way I want them to. It doesn't matter if I lose my best friend or I gain new friends. All that matters is Christ Jesus alone. I can do all things because He is the center of my life, and He has promised to take care of me."

Everyone has problems. No doubt you have a problem, a difficult situation you are facing. I ask you, "Where is your focus?"

If Jesus is the energizing center of your life, contentment is possible. It worked for Paul, and it can work for you.

6

It's Always Harder Than You Thought It Would Be

I sat in my recliner one day while recuperating from an automobile accident. I felt especially glamorous that afternoon without a bit of makeup on, gloriously donned in my old house robe, vegetating my day away. I decided to go channel-surfing — win-a-new-life game show, no; shop-til-you-drop network, no; my husband left me and my sister is making moves on my new boyfriend talk show, no; Aha! finally, good old-fashioned soap operas. OK, I admit, I gave them a try. I never was much of a soap opera fan, and that day I realized why.

As the Stomach Turns

The camera focused on a Greek god and "godette" lying next to each other in a beautifully color-coordinated Laura Ashley bedroom. Of course, these people were married — only not to each other. The woman, whose long golden hair lay perfectly splayed on the color-coordinated pillowcase, had no morning breath or little crusty things in the corners of her eyes, and her makeup was perfect.

This was the morning-after-the-night-before. Her lover was leaning over her on one elbow. Sculpted body, every *GQ* hair in place, he uttered one word: "Sapphire."

That was her name.

"Slade," she answered.

"Sapphire."

"Slade."

"Sapphire."

"Slade."

I think you get the picture.

Have you ever noticed these perfect people in their perfect houses don't have names like real people? So, here women all over the world sit watching this stuff. Except, of course, in Spain it's Juan, Bianca and so forth.

Then *your* husband comes in the door. His name naturally is not Slade, Rock or Juan — it's Herb. He comes in from work, eats dinner without speaking, belches, then falls asleep in the recliner in front of the TV. You watch your lover as his pot belly heaves up and down in concert with his snore. Hmm...he's no Slade, but of course, you're no Sapphire!

We all know the image we're sold on television is not real life. One thing I've learned about real life in my Christian walk is this: *It's always harder than you thought it would be!* It's a wilderness experience.

Why does God bring us into the wilderness? He brings us in to humble us and to show us what is in our heart if we do the will of God. Are you willing to do the will of God in the wilderness?

From A to Z With the Alpha and Omega

The entire kingdom of God can be summed up by the A to Z principle. A is the place where we begin, where we start our Christian walk; Z is the place where all the promises come to pass.

At point A, the Spirit of the Lord says to us, "Daughter, do you want to see your destiny? Do you want Me to speak and show you what I've got for you?" Our reply is, "Yes, God. I want it! I want to see it!"

He gives us a wonderful word through a prophet at a special meeting. He tells us, "Enter and possess your promise." We say, "All right, I can do that." We sing, "I am able to go up and take the country, yeah, and possess the land from Jordan to..." Hey, where did everyone go?

At point C, we find we're right in the middle of the valley of the shadow that looks like death. But we press on to points E, F and G and say, "Lord, what's going on?"

We start doing warfare. We bind everything. I used to make a religion out of binding things. "I bind you to the third and fourth degree and the fifth and seventh level. I rebuke you. The Lord bind you, Ichabod spirit."

My husband once asked, "What are you doing?"

I answered, "I'm binding."

"Why?" he said. "There's not a demon within five miles of this place. You can stop."

Then we reach points L and M. That's when we say, "Oh Jesus, just kill me. Take me home. I can't take it anymore. If it weren't for my children I could just die right now."

Jesus doesn't kill you, because the object is not to get you to heaven but to get heaven in you. If God wanted you in heaven, as soon as you got saved He would have given your pastor a gun and *bang,* he would have punched your ticket and sent you to heaven.

So the Lord lets you live. You press on until you get to R and S, and you think, "Where's that person that gave me this word? I want their name and number. I don't want any more prophecies." (I once told my husband I don't need another prophecy; if all the ones I've already received would just come to pass, I'd be set for the rest of my life.)

Finally, we get to X and Y. That's where we can say, "Lord, if You take me in and bring Your promise to pass, I'll praise Your name. If You don't bring it to pass, I'll praise Your name. All I want to do is glorify You." And then, boom! The Spirit of God takes us right into Z.

You may be thinking, Cathy, if I had known that back at point A, I'd have said, "I'll praise Your name whether You bring me in or not."

But you see, God doesn't do that, because He knows you need to go through A to Y so He can work the character of His Son in you. The person that goes into the wilderness is not the same person that comes out. It's the wilderness experience that transforms.

Lessons in the Wilderness

When Christ first comes into your life and you are born again, you have simple lessons to learn. After you have been walking with the Lord for a few years, you go into new territories and new areas, and you get to the place where things that used to work in your life don't work anymore. You learn to bind and rebuke.

You begin to say, "Lord, use me," so He begins to expand you and take you to a new level. "Have I not commanded you? Be strong and courageous. Do not be terrified; do not be discouraged, for the Lord your God will be with you wherever you go" (Josh. 1:9, NIV).

Maybe you've reached a new plateau, and it's taking a greater faith to jump to the higher plane He has for you.

Reason has started to move in and explain why God has not yet done what He promised. You tell yourself He can't do it, you are out of His will, you missed it. You wonder why you made such a stupid commitment, and suddenly, reason cuts off the head of faith.

God wants you to realize that the purpose of the lessons in the wilderness is to bring you to a place where you can say, "I *will* trust the Lord."

The older Israelites died in the wilderness. They had a fearful slave mentality. God wants to take that same fear from you, the fear that says, "I've failed and disappointed the Lord, and I know He won't bring me through this wilderness I'm facing."

God is birthing a new generation today, a generation that has made the decision to trust Him no matter what happens. I used to sing a song about being in the valley where God could restore my soul, because He knew I couldn't grow on the mountain. That's where the wilderness takes us at some point in time — in the valley.

Principles are taught in the wilderness. One principle God has taught me is that truth supersedes knowledge. There is nothing wrong with having knowledge, but I would rather have my eighty-eight-year-old grandmother, who is definitely not a scholar, lay her hands on me and release the anointing of God on my life than any learned person I know.

The same holds true for marriage. People may tell you what marriage should be like. Prince Charming rides up on his beautiful white horse, sweeps a sweet young girl off her feet and they ride off together to live happily ever after in his palace. I have said many times: "Those that wait for their knight in shining armor to come and sweep them off their feet still have to clean up after his horse." Remember, truth supersedes knowledge.

This principle applies to child rearing as well. Someone who has never had children tries to tell you how to raise yours. They really have no firsthand knowledge about how to bring up kids.

Moses had one of the best educations anyone could have. He sat under the teaching of the finest scholars. Yet, when God wanted to teach him who He was and tell him of His plan for his life, where did He take him? To the wilderness.

The wilderness is not only a place where we can see His deliverance, but also a place where we can learn. It's a place where our own formulas often fail. We tend to command God's word to come to pass, and we want it by Thursday, which is our timing, not His. God is not obligated to do our bidding just because we kick and scream and demand.

Most people would like to control every situation, but that's just not possible. Some years ago, we were planning to move. I came home from a meeting in Pittsburgh on a Friday night and had to be packed and ready to move by Monday. On Saturday I was frantically throwing things into boxes when I was informed that the deal was off, and we didn't have a house to move into.

I said, "This is it. I've had it!" I wanted to go to bed and pull the covers over my head until the whole mess was straightened out. Suddenly, I decided I was going to laugh. I certainly didn't feel like laughing, but I knew there was a lesson in this somewhere that I needed to learn. So I began to walk through the house laughing — stumbling over all the boxes, but laughing. My husband walked into the house and thought I had surely gone off the deep end.

I rejoiced and laughed and told the Lord that He was in control, and I couldn't wait to see what He was going to do. Within twenty-four hours, the entire situation was resolved. On Monday, I moved into my new house.

My first inclination had been to doubt. "Maybe this isn't the house for us, maybe God didn't want us to move, maybe...maybe..." I was willing to go wherever God wanted me to, but I was not going to bow to the enemy who tried to rob me of my peace.

Are You Tired of Being in the Classroom?

If we don't obey, we will never graduate; we'll always be in the classroom. There are some who walk through the same trials and tribulations year after year, always learning but never coming to complete knowledge. They never grow as they run from meeting to meeting, looking for a "word from the Lord."

Paul tells us in 2 Corinthians 12:7 that he had a thorn in his flesh that was a torment to him. But God told him His grace was sufficient to overcome, and in the end, Paul said that he delighted in his weaknesses, because in them, he became strong. He wasn't just barely making it; he was an overcomer.

It isn't God's plan to yank you out of your wilderness and plant you in a calm, serene place. But we want a word from God telling us the date and time we are going to be free from our pain and suffering. We don't want to deal with the problem in God's way. He wants to teach you not to scream on the battlefield.

We sing about God training our hands for war so that a bow of steel is broken in our arms. We are to become a spiritual Arnold Schwarzenegger, the Terminator. God wants to give us a backbone of steel so we won't bend under pressure.

God is looking for generals to bring courage to men and women who are on the battlefield. When the prophetic word of the Lord goes forth, that's what it does. It brings hope to those in battle and tells the wounded to hang on, because victory is near.

You drop your weapons and pick up the white flag because it's not as heavy to carry. You surrender because you think you can't make it. God wants you to pick up your weapons again.

Personal battles are a boot camp for your ministry. If you can't get victory in your household, how do you expect to get it in the outside world? Just as Abraham was an intercessor for Lot and his family when they were about to go up in smoke in Sodom and Gomorrah, God wants you to be an intercessor for His people.

Who can God trust to stand in the gap? Abraham persisted and God spared Lot. That's the kind of Christian we should strive to be, a persistent intercessor.

I had a dream that I believe was from the Lord. In it, everyone in the congregation was handed some peanuts. After I was done ministering, a love offering was taken for me. Everyone began to throw their peanuts into the basket. I tried to tell the people, "Don't do this. What you are giving to the Lord is just peanuts. God wants to take you to a greater faith level in finances."

I tried to instruct the people, but they would not listen. One by one they got up and left.

When I woke up, my pillow was soaked. I was weeping and grieving over the people and the low value they had put on the Word of God. When the word that would give them life came forth, they had other things to do and went away.

As I was grieving, the Lord spoke to me and said, "There are many in My body that are exactly like that, Cathy. They are truth rejecters; they hear it over and over again, but they are as the man that looks in the mirror and sees his image and walks away and can't remember it. They hear My Word but do not obey it or act upon what they hear."

The Wilderness Is a Lousy Campground

You may set up camp in the wilderness and cry all the time. The lessons in the wilderness are intended to get you to the other side. He wants you to walk in the plan and promise He has for you. He is continually challenging your faith so you can go to a new level in Him. It's faith that will bring you through.

Moses interceded for his people and avoided disaster. Intercession is a face-to-face relationship with God followed by persistence. It doesn't mean you have to pray three hours nonstop, but you must mean business when you pray and petition Him with His Word.

Be honest, confess your sin, and repent for the assignments that you have failed to fulfill.

I once asked the Lord why He was so good to me, knowing I have not done all that He desired for me to do. I know many better-looking, talented Christians crying to God to be used in the ministry.

The Lord answered me this way: "It's because you've put principle into practice in your life, and that is what brings the blessing. You have continually walked in obedience before Me, and that's why the blessing of the Lord is upon you."

God does not have favorites. He doesn't love any one of us more than any other. He will favor those who make Him *their* favorite and fulfill the assignment He has given them.

What is your assignment? Has He asked you to pray more, witness more — or stop worrying? You know what it is. It's not too hard. I heard a minister once say, "Inch by inch, anything's a cinch."

Oh No, Lord, Not Coffee and Sugar!

God has dealt with me about some things that you may think are unimportant. First, God showed me I had to quit drinking so much coffee because it was having an adverse effect on my body. Then, God dealt with me concerning my sugar consumption. I cut back and slowly felt better.

Then someone told me they only ate organically-grown foods. I said to myself, "Some day I am going to have an organic garden, and then I'm going to weave my own material and make my own clothes, and the wool will come from organically fed goats." *Not!*

Of course, raising organic wool is unreasonable because it's easier to go to the department store and buy ready-made everything. But what about the neighbor God has put on your heart to minister to? You've been putting that off for a long time. God wants you to stand in the gap for them, for your family and for your children that are away from Him.

The last place you feel like ministering in is the wilderness. You don't feel like encouraging someone else when you need them to minister to you. But you'll be amazed at how it will lift your spirits when you reach out to someone else and quit worrying about your own problems.

I had to learn this when Jerusha was just beginning to walk at thirteen months. She was late getting started, but made up for it very quickly.

We had been taking care of an elderly Jewish woman in our apartment complex, and I was fixing her breakfast. In the time it took for me to serve her, Jerusha had gotten into the trash can, pulled out a lid to a tin can and was running through the house. The next thing I saw was my baby sitting on the floor screaming. Blood was everywhere, I couldn't even find the wound.

An ambulance was summoned and as we rushed her to the hospital, I overheard the paramedic say to his partner, "No sense in rushing. She's lost too much blood. She'll never make it." Grabbing my daughter, I began to pray in the Spirit, cursing the spirit of death.

A surgeon was called in who, upon examining our daughter, told us the sharp lid had penetrated her right hand, severing the nerves, tendons and arteries. Microsurgery, a brand new field of medicine at the time, was going to be tried. If not successful, amputation above the wrist was suggested. My husband, Randi, looked at the compassionate surgeon and stated boldly, "We will not sign a release for amputation. You do your best

Doctor and we believe our great Physician will accomplish the rest."

After three and a half hours of surgery the doctor emerged shaking his head. "I could not not connect the severed arteries. They retracted and are so small I do not give much hope for recovery in that hand."

We were given two options: 1) she could lose the hand or fingers due to insufficient blood supply; or 2) her hand might never grow and she would never have full use of it.

During the week we were in the hospital only a few of our church family came by or called. When we returned home, a woman in the church informed us they were counseled to stay away from us. One of the members of their intercessory prayer group told them our daughter's accident was a result of our secret sin! They said God was punishing us!

I sat on the living room floor, held my baby and sobbed.

I kept hearing the words "forgive her" over and over again. God gave me the grace to face the woman and embrace her, as she cried for forgiveness. I had to minister to her even while I was in the wilderness in the midst of my grief.

You can do it too. Make Christ the energizing center of your life. Let your life revolve around Him. Take your focus off yourself. You may find yourself with a lovely attitude toward those who aren't very lovely to you.

Today our daughter's hand is whole. She has complete use of it and plays the piano with ease. The only memory she has of that ordeal is the surgeon's stitches — which form a perfect cross on her hand. I bear the same marks myself — on my heart.

7

The Reason You Want to Leave Is Probably the Reason You're There

You may have had the experience of waking up and finding out that the devil has dumped a truckload of misery all over your front yard. He's at his best when he can make you miserable.

And he has his little demons out there doing their best to add to that misery. For years, Christians didn't quite know what to do about that. Then God showed us how to do spiritual warfare, and a lot of us went off the deep end. (I don't believe there is a demon behind every rock. I believe there are *ten* demons behind every rock.)

For a while, we got so serious about demons that we forgot Revelation 19:6, which tells us that the Lord God, the omnipotent, reigns. We don't have to wait until the end to win; we could win now, today!

We have an all-powerful God who has all power for us. That doesn't mean that I'm not aware that there is an enemy, but I believe that Jesus is the light that destroys the enemy's darkness.

I heard someone once say that our spiritual warfare conferences would be shortened if we would just enter in with about six hours of praise and worship. That would mark the end of the spiritual warfare conferences, because there is not one devil that is going to stay around when people press into the holy of holies with praise and worship.

If you're torn and bent by the devil, put a worship tape in your Walkman, don your earphones, turn the volume as loud as you can stand it and begin to worship the Lord, because the enemy does not want to abide where the presence of the Lord is.

Hard Places Are Not an Option

On Mother's Day, I love getting cards not only from my own children but also from men and women that I have birthed in the Spirit of God — although some of them seem a hundred years older than I am.

That kind of relationship with your spiritual children is called mentoring. When you are ready, God will show you who you are to mentor and who should mentor you.

Now if anyone approaches you and tells you that God told them to mentor you and train you, turn and run as fast as you can. That is not the Spirit of the Lord. When God puts you with the right person, you will want what they have. They won't ask you to submit to them. You'll see something in them that you admire, and you will want the anointing that is in them.

75

Erin, who is now my secretary, called me from Washington state several years ago and told me she was selling all her personal belongings and moving to Florida, where we live. She told me she wanted what Randi and I had, and she was willing to give up everything for the kingdom of God. I listened with reservations, as I had heard similar words so many times before from other people.

She had called in May. In August she appeared on my doorstep saying, "Here I am. I want to be trained. I want to learn the things of the Spirit of the Lord."

I am not encouraging you to show up on my doorstep, but I am saying that when God puts someone in your life that has the goods, you'll do whatever it takes to have what they possess. I am not talking about following man, but about following the Spirit of God that is in man.

The apostle Paul raised many sons to follow after him in the ministry. One of them was a young man named Titus. He was Paul's son in the Lord, and his missionary responsibility was a place called Crete. Crete is not a very pleasant place to live. It was Titus's first missionary trip. Paul said, "I am sending you to Crete to establish a work in that place" (see Titus 1:5).

You no doubt have heard of someone being called a Cretan, and you thought it meant someone from outer space. Paul heard a report from one of the prophets from Crete, who basically said, "I'm telling you, I am one of their own and I am telling you they are lousy, they are liars, deceivers, lazy, gluttons and they are actually worthless. They go from house to house, they receive false doctrine, they do it for filthy gain. They are Balaams. They are my own people and I am ashamed of them" (see Titus 1:10-12).

That was the description of the Cretan people. Paul sent Titus there and said, "For this cause I left thee in Crete" (Titus 1:5). Crete was a place of problems.

Paul himself never avoided hard places. He was beaten, shipwrecked, bound and abased. I love to read about the time Paul went into the city of Lystra to preach the gospel (see Acts 14:19-20). The Jews dragged him outside the city, beat him and left him for dead. God raised him up, and he went back into the city and began preaching again.

God is putting together a people who, like Paul, will not shrink from the hard places.

Can You Top This?

I grew up thinking I knew all about the hard places. When I was a child, Sunday night was usually testimony night at the little Pentecostal church in Florida where my father pastored. I hated it. No matter how many times my dad asked the people to keep it short and not tell of *their* achievements, it was to no avail. Invariably, people would always end with, "Please pray for me that I'll endure to the end."

The only thing that outdid testimony night was when my father asked for prayer requests. It sounded like a rerun of the old radio program *Can You Top This?* "My mother, sister, aunts, uncles, dogs and niece have a fever and I'm afraid I'm going to get it and die. You all pray and I'll give the glory to God in Jesus' name." You get the picture.

The topper was when a young woman asked for prayer about her "female problems" and went into a detailed description of her recent visit to the gynecologist. I watched my mother's face turn crimson. She looked at my dad with pleading eyes hoping he could somehow shut the woman up. I was sitting in the back of the church, looking at my brother and thinking, "Is this what we have to look forward to? Pray that I endure to the end!"

Paul didn't shrink from the hard places. His attitude was, "Lord, enlarge me and my capacity to be an example for You." That's what the Spirit of the Lord wants to do in us.

Crete was a hard place, and the Cretans were a bad lot of people. It wasn't just the backsliders; the *Christians* couldn't even get their act together. Allow me to use my imagination and paraphrase the letter from Titus to Paul.

> I really respect you and I really honor your wisdom, but I am so miserable. Would you please do me a favor and get me out of here? There are a lot of lousy people in here, and I am just a young man. This is too hard for me. Bring me back to Jerusalem, if you don't mind, please. Let me just be an associate pastor some place where I don't have to take the heat.

Paul wrote back and said, "For this reason, Titus, I left you in Crete." Let me paraphrase again. Paul said,

> Yes, I know it's a terrible place. I know they are terrible people. You're right in everything you said, Titus. There is a tremendous need in Crete. All the reasons you said you wanted to leave are all the reasons that I sent you there to begin with.

Are you in Crete, the hard place, the place of problems, the place where it seems that everyone around you doesn't do right no matter how you witness to them and give them your best testimony? We are different in many ways, but one thing I know, all of us have either been in Crete, are going to be in Crete, or are in Crete right now.

You ask me not to make that confession over you. It doesn't matter if we confess it or not. Crete, like the wilderness, is not an option. The only option is how long you stay there. Deuteronomy tells us that the wilderness comes to humble and test you, to see what is in your heart. God must do that before He can give you your promise.

We are all human, and when we find ourselves in Crete our first response is, "I want out! Lord, if You love me, why did You let this happen to me? I know the devil did it, but You could have prevented it." We begin to launch into our "It's not fair" thing.

Whining in the Valley

I wonder what Titus thought when he got Paul's response. I hear people say, "I am far too talented to be left here. I'm far too valuable to be put on the back side of the desert. I'm being wasted in this place. Cathy, you just don't understand how hard it is. At least your husband is a Christian. You don't know what it's like being married to an unbeliever. I am all alone, and all I have is my antidepressant pill to get me through."

I've just about heard it all. There is a woman who calls me all the time with the same story: "Nobody knows how hard it is for me." She tells me of her pain, the worst she's ever had. I remind her that she said that yesterday, but she assures me that today it's worse.

I know all about trials and wildernesses. There are two things I have learned through them. First, everybody's got trials; second, they are temporary. The valley and the wilderness are not places where you dwell permanently.

Back in the old Pentecostal days, we thought the valley was the normal Christian life. We sang songs like, "Farther along we'll know all about it, farther along we'll understand why." And my favorite: "Cheer up, my brother. While you're here you're a poor miserable worm, but when we all get to heaven, what a day of rejoicing that will be." (At least that's what it sounded like to me.)

The only time we got excited was when we sang, "I'll Fly Away,"(oh glory!). I remember one dear sister who would take off running around the church. She was the one at the midweek service who would ask us to pray that she would endure to the end.

The valley of the shadow of death isn't where we're supposed to live. The Word says, "Yea, though I walk through the valley" (Ps. 23:4). If you sit down and whine and complain, you will still be in your valley a year from now.

You say your relationship, your job, your marriage, your church or wherever you are is too hard? Happiness is not something that you stumble on. Happiness is something you decide you are going to have right where you are, even if you are in your Crete.

Granted, you may not always have genuine happiness, but you can always have joy. You can create joy right where you are. The joy of the Lord really can be your strength; God will help you in your Crete if you seek Him daily.

The Leftovers May Be From God

I once heard a well-known pastor say that he prays in the Spirit one hour a day, over and above his regular prayer time. I thought that I would really be anointed if I prayed in tongues for an hour, nonstop, every day.

Now, when you're not used to doing something, it's like exercising. Example: I have Richard Simmons' exercise video *Sweatin' to the Oldies.* The first time I exercised along with the video, I knew God didn't really want me to do it, because I couldn't make it past five minutes into the program. But I persevered, and now I've graduated to the next two Richard Simmons videos. I can bounce with the best of them.

That's the way it is when you first go into your prayer closet. I started with what seemed like forever. It was ten minutes. I gradually increased my prayer time until I reached that hour. I really love my time alone with the Lord now.

But back to Crete. The worst thing about Crete is disillusionment. Compare it to a bride and groom after six months of marriage; it's nothing like what they thought it would be. Or ask a young person in the middle of boot camp how things are going: "I thought I was going to get a color-coordinated outfit, some good food and a paycheck. I didn't know it was going to be like this."

That's disillusionment. You may have stood, believed and

confessed a word from the Lord. When it didn't turn out the way you thought it would, you found yourself in the middle of Crete.

Crete can be an opportunity for you, just as it was for Titus. So many times we look at the difficult situations we are in and can't see what good can come of them. If you stand your ground, you will see the glory of God visit you in your season of need. That which He promises, He will do, because He cannot lie. He will fulfill His word to you.

In the very place that Titus wanted to escape from, God established him. "For this cause I left you in Crete." To do what? To set in order what remains.

When I was in Central America, lying on the floor unable to sleep, I got out my little battery-operated flashlight and began to read the Word. The Lord made this phrase so real to me, "to set in order what remains" — in other words what's leftover.

Do you really know what leftovers are? I'm sure most of you can relate to this scenario: On Thanksgiving Day, after you have spent three days baking pies, you cook that turkey and all the trimmings. You've set your table and it looks beautiful.

The family comes in like a bunch of locusts and devours it all in thirty minutes. Then all of a sudden, when they are finished, they develop a headache, have to go to the bathroom (which my mom says was my favorite line) or have an appointment they must keep.

After three days of hard labor and thirty minutes of eating, there you sit, staring at a turkey carcass, half-eaten yams and all that crusty baked-on stuff on your Corningware casserole dishes. Those are the remains — what is leftover after the best is gone.

Paul said, "For this reason I left you in Crete." To do what? That you might strengthen, build up and straighten out the remains, the mess, the leftovers, the lives of the broken, the shattered, the wounded, the teens that have walked in rebellion and have been on drugs; all those who have reached bottom.

Jesus is so unlike man. He doesn't take only the best. He takes the ones that are considered throwaways as well.

How to Get Out

Maybe you have realized that you're in Crete and now your question is, "How do I get out?" The first thing to do is quit trying to figure out *how* you got there, in other words don't visit the past. The enemy will try to tell you it's all your fault that you are where you are because of things that happened in the past.

Next, don't start looking for the first boat off the island. You may miss the "luau" and the most important lesson you've ever learned. The Lord has taught me quite a lot in Crete, probably more than any other time in my life.

Another important thing to remember is to rely on God's Word, not your feelings. The Lord has put the blueprints to life in the Bible. The answers we search for are on those pages. We can't rely on our feelings.

Finally, we must let the Lord take the "no" out of us. The no is the thing that causes you to shrug your shoulders and say, "I don't want to do what You ask of me, Lord." Let the Spirit of God bring you to the place where you are willing to say, "Lord, this is what I desire with all my heart. You gave me the promise. Nevertheless, not my will but Thine be done."

Whatever God is dealing with you about — whether it be submitting to someone who is a hard taskmaster, a marriage that you feel you have every right to run away from, or your job that you want to quit — submit to Him in your Crete.

We all have our own personal Crete, and it is real. How can you keep Crete from becoming your enemy? I believe that after you have bound everything and the situation doesn't change, it just may be God. After I've bound, rebuked, fasted and prayed and it still doesn't go away, I have to believe that I'm exactly where God wants me.

As you look for an escape from Crete, do you know what God is saying to you? Don't run, stay in your Crete, pray in your Crete. Build up the lives of the broken and hurting and wounded. He is telling you to hang in there; He wants to do something in that hard place.

8

You Win or Lose by the Way You Choose

There are witches in the back of the auditorium, waiting for the service to start." Those were the words the Costa Rican pastor spoke to me as we sat in his office before going into a service.

"How could he be so calm?" I thought. All I could see in my mind's eye were these witches sitting in the back of the church sticking pins in their Cathy dolls, saying, "The eyes, the eyes!" What I didn't know was that this congregation was used to having witches in the services.

Reason told me to run the other way, but faith said, "Go in

and minister to these people who are hungry for the Word of God." With all that was within me, I tried to block the witches from my mind and began to give the people what God had placed in my heart.

We had a glorious service and many were saved, healed and delivered. However, I noticed something unusual as I began to do personal ministry at the end of the service. Many Christians who were in the service formed a single line in front of the platform area with arms linked together, praying in the Spirit.

After the service, I asked the pastor where the witches were. He said, "They left when they saw a wall of fire all across the front of the platform."

When we've been walking with Jesus a long time, the battles don't subside; they grow greater. I've said it before: "New levels bring new devils." If you're waiting for a time when you won't be attacked, forget it. That time is never going to come.

You Are What You Think

Wherever you go, you bring the kingdom of God. For born-again, Spirit-filled children, there is one thing that will hinder us from possessing the perfect will of God, and it sits on top of our shoulders.

"For as he thinketh in his heart, so is he" (Prov. 23:7). Your condition right now is a result of what *you* did yesterday, last month or last year. It is not a result of your mother's mother's mother who used to persecute dogs. Now you're here, and you need inner healing.

When I was believing for God to bless me with a baby, someone gave me a cradle filled with beautiful, new baby clothes. You would not believe the baby stuff I accumulated over the years. It just kept coming in. All I needed was a baby.

I had to choose. I said, "Lord, it seems as if it's always later, never now." Ever felt like that? "Yeah, yeah, God's going to give me a new car. He'll pour His glory out — later, not now."

The word of the Lord says now, now, now. Once when I walked into my living room and saw that cradle filled with all those little things, I wanted to shout, "Get it out of here!" Then I said, "No, bless God, it's going to sit in the middle of my living room until I put my baby in it."

Victory is a matter of changing our minds about what we choose to believe.

> Therefore, I urge you, brothers, in view of God's mercy, to offer your bodies as living sacrifices holy and pleasing to God — which is your spiritual worship. Do not conform any longer to the pattern of this world, but be transformed by the renewing of your mind (Rom. 12:1-2, NIV).

How? You transform your whole body. You transform your household situation. You transform your finances. You transform your job. You transform everything by the renewing of your mind. "For as he thinketh in his heart, so is he" (Prov. 23:7). You transform everything in your life by getting your mind saved and renewing it. Then you will be able to test and approve what is the will of God, His good and perfect will.

Molded or Moldy?

Many Christians are conformed to this world. Conformed means molded. We are molded into the world's form, but God is smashing molds. The Lord says when we come to Him He will mold us but not to the world's form. There are a lot of Christians that still think like unsaved people. Their lives are based on their feelings, their experience, the economy, their job and the natural elements.

We, as Christians, are to be transformed by the renewing of our minds, and our entire life is supposed to be based on what the Word of God says. That's difficult to grasp because many of us have been trained our entire lives to depend on our feelings.

Church people used to say that you could tell how good a service was by how many bobby pins Sister So-and-So still had in her hair when the service was over and how many pins were on the floor. Yet, for all the jumping and shouting, there was no change in the people's lives. They shouted on Sunday, but they were depressed on Monday.

It's not the shout that God is looking for. He wants to transform your mind. If your life is based on the joy of circumstances, all the devil has to do is serve you a couple of bad circumstances. Let your husband yell at you, let the kids get bad grades, let your boss say something to upset you, get stuck in traffic or have a flat tire and all of a sudden, he's finished you off for the rest of the day. You walk around depressed.

One day when I thought I was on top of things, we received a phone call from a man who lambasted our ministry. He really let us have it. I let those comments get into my spirit, and I stewed about it all day. I rehearsed what I should have said to him in response. Why didn't I think of those things while he was on the phone instead of after he hung up?

We get upset and start slamming doors, banging cupboards and yell at the kids. Instead of listening to what the Word of God tells us to do, we let the situation roll around in our brain. We give it the power to tell us how we are going to feel. It happens to baby Christians and seasoned ones alike. The enemy is there to come against the Word of God. Therefore, we have to continually renew our minds.

As I fumed about that phone call, the Lord spoke to me and said, "Cathy, you're doing the very things you're going to preach against tomorrow." I had to renew my mind and block out all the ugliness caused by one phone call.

Recently, after a meeting in Philadelphia, I was at the airport already when I realized I had left my cassette tapes and my Walkman in the nightstand drawer at the hotel. I called the hotel, and the household staff vowed there were no tapes or Walkman in that room. A pastor even went back to check, and sure enough they were gone. But, of course, no one took them!

This may sound like no big deal to you, but at the time I could not fly without my Walkman. It was my crutch. It blocked out airplane sounds and kept the plane in the air. I began to panic, because now I could hear every sound, and our plane didn't look very sturdy to me. To make matters worse as we taxied down the runway, the lady behind me was hyperventilating, saying, "Dear God, we're moving. I knew we shouldn't have flown. We'll never make it. What's that sound?"

Her husband didn't help any when he said, "I hope somebody prayed this morning." My mother calmly worked her crossword puzzles.

I heard the Lord speak to me all the way home, "Change your mind about what you think. You don't need your Walkman. All you need is Me." We have to change our thoughts, if what we are thinking contradicts the Word of God.

> "For my thoughts are not your thoughts, neither are your ways my ways," declares the Lord. "As the Heavens are higher than the earth, so are my ways higher than your ways and my thoughts than your thoughts" (Is. 55:8-9, NIV).

I have to exchange my thoughts for His thoughts. I have to change the way I feel. If I found a flaw in a dress I just bought, I would go back to the store and tell them I wanted another dress. What would they want in exchange? The damaged dress for the new one.

That's how you have to renew your mind. You have to exchange the problem for God's thoughts. As Christians, we must decide that we want God's thoughts.

There's Just No Substitute for Renewing Your Mind

My mother loves all those exercise contraptions that they advertise on TV. One hotel where we stayed had a wonderful exercise room. We decided to take advantage of it, so I got on the bicycle, and my mom got on the rowing machine.

I asked her if she had ever done anything like that before. She said, "No, but I can handle it." The only problem is that she is Italian and she has these little short legs.

When I was ready to leave, I heard a muffled cry, "Cathy, Cathy!" Now, here is this room full of executives doing their thing. I couldn't help but laugh as I looked at her. She was sitting there with tears running down her cheeks. "I'm stuck. I can't get up." Her little short Italian legs were stuck under the oars.

She once had a gadget that you hook onto the door knob. You work these pulleys back and forth with your arms and legs, and you're guaranteed to have a flat stomach in thirty minutes. That lasted one week.

My husband even fell for some of this stuff. He bought some grapefruit pills that you take at bedtime, and by morning, like magic, you're ten pounds lighter. It had to be true, because the ad showed a woman who had lost tons of weight. Needless to say, we have a half bottle of grapefruit pills sitting on the shelf because the stuff just doesn't work. Only one way to do it...stop eating and exercise.

We buy tapes and books that are supposed to change our lives, make us look better, make us rich overnight. We love that stuff because it's instantaneous. But even with all the self-help stuff we have, there is no change because there is only one self-help book that works — the Bible.

The Word of God is the greatest self-help book there is. Study it, get it in you and it will change you. You'll find that the very thing you don't want to change or renew in your mind is the very thing that will keep you from walking in the blessing.

Ever Hear of Pride of the Mind?

There is nothing in us as hard to change as the pride of the mind. I have counseled people and told them what I was sensing in the Holy Spirit. The response I get most often is, "Yes, but..."

There are people who sit and listen to counsel, but they're thinking, "You can say what you want, but I know I heard God and I'm not receiving this." That's the pride of the mind. You can check on them six months later, and they are still in the same situation. Why? Because we have to humble ourselves and hear what the Spirit of the Lord is saying. His ways are higher than our ways.

The apostle Paul said we are not to give place to the devil. One version says not to give a toe-hold to the devil. All Satan needs is to get a toe-hold in one unprotected area that is not wholly surrendered to God.

My husband is so good for me along those lines. When I begin to complain, he won't let me finish. He'll say, "You're judging." I want to tell him to just be quiet and let me tell him how miserable I am. I want my right to rehearse how bad my situation is. I have to repent right then or I know I'm going to get message number 323 from him about keeping my heart right.

Every area of our lives has to be surrendered to God's thinking. It's not enough to surrender on the outside; we've got to surrender on the inside. We've got to circumcise our stubborn hearts.

You and your husband get into a heated discussion, and he says something you don't like. You say, "I'm just saying this one thing." He responds; you answer, "I'm going to make this one last statement."

The Holy Spirit is saying to you, "Shut up, shut up, shut up!" You tell Him, "I will in a minute, but I have one last thing I've got to say." We turn that deaf ear to the Lord. We are used to saying what we please, even though the Holy Spirit is prompting us to be quiet and let Him work in the situation.

We work so hard not to confess the negative, but we know that out of the abundance of our heart, our mouth speaks. If it's in your heart, it's going to come out of your mouth. If you change your heart and mind, then the right words will come out of your mouth.

Why do our words have such effect? Because we are created in the image of the One whose words created the universe.

> Let us make man in our image, in our likeness, and let them rule over the fish of the sea, [I remember that every time I swim in the ocean: "Jaws, you are under my feet"] and the birds of the air, over the livestock, over all the earth, and over all the creatures that move along the ground (Gen. 1:26, NIV).

There are many eternal spirits. There are angels, and there are demons. The Bible doesn't say they are created in the image of the likeness of God. You are created in the image and likeness of God. The angels do the will of the Father, but we are sovereign over our own lives.

You Make the Decision

"The devil made me do it!" Those are words we should never say, even though there is a true and valid ministry of deliverance that we need to have operating in our lives.

If you need deliverance, get it. I don't care if the demon is in you, on you, around you or if you cough it up, spit it up, or yawn it out. It doesn't matter where it is. You are sovereign over your own life. Sovereign means independent of all else.

I'm going to say something radical. God is not in control of your life.

This day I call heaven and earth as witnesses against you that I have set before you life and death, blessings and curses. Now choose life, so that you and your children may live (Deut. 30:19, NIV).

You are not just making decisions for yourself. You are making decisions for your children. God does not decide if we are blessed or cursed. We decide.

Our will is so powerful that if you choose to spend eternity in hell, you can. God will not stop you from choosing to go to hell when you die.

Jesus said, "I set before you life and death, but men love death rather than life" (see John 3:19). Many Christians pray, "Lord, whatever you want, let it just be your will." I don't think God even acknowledges those kinds of prayers.

We were taught in the church to pray, "Not my will but thine be done." I've said many times, "Lord, I choose to go. If you don't want me to, you have ways of stopping me."

God Stops, the Devil Hinders

The only time we pray a prayer of dedication and consecration is when we surrender to the Lord for either ministry or family. Jesus surrendered His ministry and life to God. When He was in the boat and grieving for His cousin John the Baptist — who had been beheaded — He didn't say, "Oh Father, if it's your will that I go, I will." He saw the need and went ashore and began to heal the people and minister to their needs.

The choice is in your heart and in your mouth. You choose: life or death, blessing or cursing.

"I wish I had never married you. I wish you were dead. I wish I was dead."

Have you ever thought those words? That's the kind of thing spouses say to each other in the heat of an argument. But words such as those — even if they're not meant literally —

plant the seeds of future doubt and marital disruption. They have a greater destructive impact than people realize.

It is so important that we take care of what we allow to come out of our mouth. The Word says, "Let the words of my mouth...be acceptable in thy sight, O Lord" (Ps. 19:14).

I recently admonished a dear sister because she prophesied her own death. Her words were, "It would be better if I were dead." I asked her to not let those destructive words come out of her mouth.

Many times when we go through trials, the enemy uses our emotions to make his moves. The words you speak will determine if you are going to triumph or not.

After any great win, the enemy will come to test you and rob you of your victory. I find that I am usually attacked by the devil about three days before I am to minister. I was preparing for a ministry trip to North Carolina, when right before I left, we had a plumbing problem. We found out that our homeowners' insurance covered everything but this type of problem. It was going to cost us about $1,200 to fix it. Then my daughter started throwing up. I laid awake the night before the trip, thinking about the plumber's bill, the clean-up and the guilt over leaving a sick child. Satan mercilessly uses unexpected circumstances to move our minds into fear.

One of the ways the enemy tries to distract or impede is to cause an argument just before we leave for church. It never fails. Your husband may have ten clean, ironed shirts hanging in the closet, but he wants the one in the laundry basket. You've just dressed the kids, and you wonder why chocolate milk stains are all over their clean clothes. And what a time to get a run in your panty hose. Now you're ready to leave, and the baby throws up all over your new dress.

You finally give up and say, "I'm not going to go to church. I'll stay home and watch my television pastor." That's an ultimate goal of the devil's. He is getting what he wants when you choose not to spend time with the Lord.

We often hear people say, "Well, I'm just waiting on the Lord." I know what God wants me to do. He has called me to set people free. I don't have to pray and cry and ask God if He wants me to minister. Our prayer should be, "Lord, flow through me. Let your anointing be on me."

Likewise, we don't have to ask God if He wants us to give. Our prayer should be, "Lord, how much?"

You will see that what you end up with in life is a matter of your choices all through life. *You win or lose by the way you choose.*

Once you change your mind and decide, "Lord, I'm going to believe it even though everything within me is screaming, 'I can't; it won't work; it's not happening'," He will do the impossible. God makes up the lack!

> Delight yourself in the Lord and he will give you the desires of your heart.
>
> Commit your way to the Lord; trust in him and he will do this:
>
> He will make your righteousness shine like the dawn, the justice of your cause like the noonday sun (Ps. 37:4-6, NIV).

Arm Yourself Before the Battle

Once my father, Clive, and my mother and I were preparing to leave Honduras for Costa Rica. My heart sank as we boarded the plane that looked like it was built by Wilbur Wright. I was further dismayed when the pilot came on board with a live, noisy chicken in a mesh bag and made his way to the cockpit. I envisioned this chicken with goggles as his co-pilot. My only hope was that he clucked in Spanish.

Flying over Nicaragua we encountered a violent storm with heavy turbulence and lightning. The more the plane shook, the louder I prayed and the faster my mother worked her crossword puzzles. I glanced at my dad across the aisle and he was sound asleep!

I was very irritated with him because he slept and left me alone to do all the praying in order to keep the plane from going down. I confronted him and his response to me was, "Cathy, I prayed this morning and the Lord assured me that the God who sent us was well able to keep us." The valuable lesson I learned from him is that the time to prepare your mind for battle is *before* the war begins!

Receive Your Fresh Start

Maybe you know what it's like to be oppressed in your mind. You have chains and are in bondage. You have been walking in torment. The enemy has planted thoughts in you that are contrary to the Word of God, and you have been in a great battle.

You can't sleep at night because fear has risen in your mind and has tried to divide your heart. You have been confused and worried.

> Therefore I tell you, whatever you ask for in prayer, believe that you have received it, and it will be yours (Mark 11:24, NIV).

If you will allow Him to, the Lord will give you a fresh start right now. He will break the bondage so that you can walk free. You will be able to say, "As for me and my house, we choose to walk with the Lord" (Josh. 24:15).

9

If You Don't Overcome Fear, It Will Overcome You

hile speaking at a series of meetings in Philadelphia, I was prompted by the Holy Spirit to call forward those who were bound by the spirit of fear and intimidation. As I stepped down from the platform to pray for those who came to the front, I was drawn to a couple in the back of the room who were both weeping and worshipping the Lord. Calling the couple forward, I heard the Lord speak these words to my heart: "Say to them, 'Do not be afraid! Even tonight you shall have your answer; before you get home tonight the new job offer will come. It will be an increase and a reward from the hand of your Father.' "

By faith I spoke this word of prophecy to them. After the meeting that night I went to Denny's with this couple. I listened as they told me everything they were going through. The husband had been working under terrible conditions and left his job. And to make matters worse, the wife was pregnant, due with the baby any day. They were so afraid of not being able to provide for the baby and meet their other expenses. Before we left we prayed and they agreed to trust in the word from the Lord.

The wife called me the next day bursting with excitement. She told me when they got home after Denny's they listened to their answering machine messages, and lo and behold there was a message from a company offering the husband a job — with a pay raise! Praise God for the accuracy of His word!

The purpose and provision of prophecy is to give hope and encouragement to a person and to reveal the mind, heart and will of God so that through faith the promise becomes a reality. One of the greatest weapons Satan will use against you to keep you from coming into that promise is *fear.*

Through the study of the Word, as well as through personal experience, I have discovered that fear is a paralyzer. *You will either overcome or be overcome by fear.*

Fear is a spirit: "For God hath not given us the spirit of fear; but of power, and of love and of a sound mind" (2 Tim. 1:7). It's a liar and a spirit without a body. If you agree with fear, fear will take up residence with you. If you agree with fear, it will become your master, and you will make decisions based on your fears.

What does fear look like? Is it embodied in the images seen in the frightening movies that are so rampant today? Is fear scary Halloween celebrations and sounds that go "bump" in the night? Fear is certainly behind those things, as their object is to frighten you, but fear is much more insidious than that.

Three Weeks of Ugly

I was raised in a Christian home. My father and mother are Assemblies of God ministers. They pastored for many years and are now involved in missionary evangelism. Despite my upbringing, an unrelenting spirit of fear would often come against me, and I would cry out to God to set me free.

My freedom came in an unlikely time and place. For the first time, I was invited to minister on my own, without my husband. I was all excited. After packing my jungle Liz-wear and coordinating outfits in my brand new luggage, I headed for the Philippines with a friend who had never been out of Florida.

We traveled three days — without changing clothes — to get to one of the hottest places on the face of the earth. Three days in the same underwear is enough to make anyone irritable.

Finally, we arrived at the home of the pastor who had extended the invitation. I knew I was in trouble when I realized I had more luggage than he had living room. Looking forward to a quick shower to improve my disposition, I mentioned I was hot and needed to bathe. He took me to another room and said, "This barrel you wash, this barrel you rinse," as he handed me a dipper. Later, I pulled out my electric rollers and asked the pastor's wife where I could plug them in. She said, "Oh, a blower!" I realized then that I was facing three weeks of ugly.

The pastor and his wife gave us their room, and I use that term loosely. I sat on the bed — also a loose term — in my slip feeling very un-Marilyn-Hickey-like. I said, "God, I can't stand it. This isn't anything like I thought it was going to be."

I could hear the Holy Spirit laughing in my ear. He said, "And you thought I brought you here to change someone else!" The Lord then gave me this scripture: "I will remove from this city those who rejoice in their pride. Never again will you be haughty on my holy hill. But I will leave within you the meek and humble, who trust in the name of the Lord. The remnant of Israel will do no wrong; they will speak no lies, nor will deceit be found in their mouths. They will eat and lie down and no one will make them afraid" (Zeph. 3:11-13, NIV).

During those three weeks the Lord dealt with me concerning my image and how unimportant it was to Him. I ministered to and among those precious Filipinos including the pastor and his wife and witnessed such a humility and purity in their worship and service to the Lord. Even with the poorest of living conditions and lack of material goods, their devotion shamed me. Upon returning home I could see how the Lord had dealt with a root of pride. In the ensuing days I noticed that situations that used to cause a tremendous response of fear no longer bound me in that fear. I was free! When the pride was dealt with, the fear left.

Ruled by Fear

As I travel, I see many precious born-again, Spirit-filled Christians who are still ruled by fear. They are afraid of economic failure, the threat of a job loss, cancer and heart attacks. They are Christians who are living a life controlled by questions such as, What if...? What will I do? or What if God *doesn't...?* What will I do?

Never forget that "they overcame him by the blood of the Lamb, and by the word of their testimony; and they loved not their lives unto the death" (Rev. 12:11). The operative word is *overcame.* Jesus, through His death and resurrection, has already made you an overcomer!

I myself struggled many years with fear, crying out to the Lord to be set free. The spirit of fear had dominated me in so many areas. I was insecure, afraid to fly, suffered from claustrophobia and eventually the fear of death. I was deceived and served fear because I had let it become my master. I didn't know at that time these principles that I am going to share with you.

Below is a list of some of the problems Christians struggle with that may be rooted in the spirit of fear.

1. Nightmares and sleeplessness

> How are they brought into desolation, as in a moment! they are utterly consumed with terrors.
> As a dream when one awaketh; so, O Lord, when thou awakest, thou shalt despise their image (Ps. 73:19-20).

2. Inability to accept the Father's perfect love (see I John 4:18)

I know many precious believers who always feel that God is mad at them, that they have somehow crossed a line that has disappointed Him one too many times. If it wasn't for Jesus, the Father would kill them! Remember that "God so loved the world, that he gave" (John 3:16). Our Father knew who and what we were when He called us, saved us and chose us. Rest in the fact that He loves us with such a great love that He gave the only Son He had for our redemption. He's not going to give up on us that easily!

3. Fear of man (see Prov. 29:25)

Are you one of those who does not obey the Holy Spirit when He leads you to witness or prophesy because you're afraid of what people will say? There are saints who will never fulfill the call of God on their lives, because of the fear of rejection by others.

4. Timidity and shyness

Some consider shyness an endearing quality. But just ask someone who has suffered from timidity and has had to stand in front of a crowd with his knees knocking, heart pounding and palms sweating, whether the pain he feels is cute or endearing.

5. Torment

I believe 90 percent of our battles are fought in the mind. A woman once asked me to pray for her, and as I did, the Lord showed me a steel band around her head becoming progressively tighter and tighter. The Holy Spirit spoke a word of knowledge to me that she had been suffering from a spirit of fear. I took authority over the spirit of fear and torment and commanded it to leave. I spoke a word of prophecy to her: "The migraine headaches will cease. The continual mind torment, from the time you wake up in the morning until you go to bed at night, has been broken off of you." She came back to report a freedom from the fear and the pain she had lived with for fifteen years.

6. Perfectionism

Mary's sister Martha was consumed with the details of life. Little has changed since then. There's so much pressure on women to fulfill all of their responsibilities to family, job, church and home. It's a rare individual who can do it all well, let alone perfectly.

In our family, we have a few simple "house rules" that keep us rejoicing and also remind us that eternal priorities are what matters. One such rule is: "Never rejoice too much when you do the last load of laundry." Why? Because with five children — four under the age of two — it won't be long before the laundry stacks right up the side of the wall again!

A second rule is: "Never rejoice too much after all the glass tabletops are clean." Reason: see above.

Trying to control every situation in order to have a perfect house, perfect children and a perfect life will eventually cause you to pull fistfuls of hair out of your head — not to mention the fact that you'll lose your joy and your ability to enjoy what God has given you.

Ask yourself, "In the light of eternity, will this really matter?"

7. Anxiety, tension and stress

> There were they in great fear, where no fear was: for God hath scattered the bones of him that encampeth against thee: thou hast put them to shame, because God hath despised them (Ps. 53:5).

Fear is no fun; just ask someone who has ever suffered a panic attack. Scripture tells us not to be anxious for anything. Freedom from anxiety is a decision, a decree and a deliverance.

The psalmist even warned us not to be afraid of "nothing." We all know people who are afraid when there is nothing to be worried about. They lie awake at night, losing sleep worrying about what they have to do the next day. What a waste of time.

Anxiety, tension and stress can also open the door for many sicknesses and diseases. Jesus, the Great Physician, says that in the last days men's hearts would fail them because of fear (see Luke 21:26).

8. Excessive carefulness

For many of us, our mothers constantly told us to be careful. My mother repeatedly told me, "Be careful to wear clean underwear, in case you're in an accident. Be careful not to step in a puddle or you'll get polio." (I even tried to use that one against her when I didn't want to take a bath.)

We equate being careful with being responsible. We are told, "You can't be too careful, you know. God helps those who help themselves."

The only problem with that advice is that it is contrary to the Word, which tells us to "be careful for nothing" (Phil. 4:6). Paul was talking about fear and anxiety. He was saying, "Stop living your life ruled by the anxiety, fear and pressure your cares bring."

Fearlessness Is a Destroyer

Now, I have great news for you! God has not given us a spirit of fear but a spirit of boldness.

> The wicked flee when no man pursueth: but the righteous are as bold as a lion (Prov. 28:1).

My husband Randi, myself and our secretary, Erin, stopped for gas late one night while returning from a ministry trip. Up roared two cars, loaded with teenage boys and stereo speakers larger than the cars. As their rock music blared, they tried to cut us off at the pump by pulling their cars in front and in back of us, trapping us in between them. My husband continued to fill the car as the boys began taunting him.

Even as they pulled out knives, baseball bats and chains, Randi assured the gang he didn't want any trouble.

"We're going to cut you, man," one boy shouted. I might note here that I wanted to quietly jump in the car, throw out my purse as a sacrifice and roll up the window as I sped away.

But that's me. However, it's definitely not my husband.

Randi walked toward this menacing group, pointed his finger at them and said, "I rebuke that demon spirit in the name of Jesus, and I claim every one of you for Jesus Christ and His kingdom."

Suddenly, the boys in this demon-crazed gang started yelling, "Leave us alone! Leave us alone!" With that they jumped in their cars and sped off. My husband jumped in our car and gave chase.

"What are you doing?" I screamed in disbelief.

"I'm going to get their license numbers and report them to the police. Why should we allow that spirit to rule over this city?"

At that point I believe I uttered something like, "Uh, huh!" and then swallowed my tongue.

My husband was doing the opposite of what fear was telling him to do. That's the essence of fearlessness.

What does fearlessness look like? True fearlessness is neither brash nor arrogant, rude nor boastful. The Word, in fact, provides numerous descriptions of a fearless Christian. Here are just a few:

1. Full of anticipation (Titus 2:13)
2. Calm (Ps. 107:29)
3. Decisive (Joel 3:14)
4. Encouraged (Judg. 20:22)
5. Confident (Is. 30:15)
6. Full of faith (Rom. 4:20)
7. Strong-hearted (Ps. 31:24)
8. Accepted by God (Eph. 1:6)
9. Peaceable (Is. 32:18)
10. Tranquil (Dan. 4:27)
11. Trusting (Ps. 56:11)
12. Possessing a sound mind (2 Tim. 1:7)
13. Compassionate (Jude 22)
14. Disciplined (1 Cor. 9:25)
15. Bold (Phil. 1:8)

Oh, that we would walk in all the provision Jesus died to give us! Joel 3:16 says: "The Lord also shall roar out of Zion." You and I are a spiritual Zion, and the Lord desires to roar out of us just as a lion roars! Speak out against or "roar out" at these fears that have kept you in physical, spiritual and emotional bondage.

We have read that perfect love casts out fear. In my own life as I battled fear and all of its symptoms, one thing I realized was not an established fact in my life. Jesus loved me! Sometimes I thought I knew how far my heavenly Father was committed to go for me, then the rest was up to me. The problem with that way of thinking is that it was contrary to God's Word.

Depending upon the depth and grip that fear has had on your life determines the measure of immersing your head into His Word. Your mind will resist at first, but as you continue to persevere in God's Word, your mind will wave the flag of surrender to God's Word.

Are you bound by the spirit of fear? Pray this prayer with me:

> Lord Jesus, I thank You for the price You paid for my liberty. Forgive me for serving the spirit of fear. Fear, I will serve you no more. I stand in my authority and upon the blood of the Lamb and God's Word, and I command you to go. Give me Your grace, Lord, to walk daily in boldness for the building of Your kingdom. In Jesus' name, amen.

10

Rejected on the Assembly Line of Life

Have you ever felt like God rejected you, and He was a million miles away because you had done something to disappoint Him? I believe latest statistics say about 1.4562 zillion Christians have felt that way at one time. I know I felt that way for years before the Lord delivered me. I used to think I was the only one who struggled with rejection until I received a visit one day from the "perfect" pastor's wife.

She was everything I always tried to be but couldn't attain — tall, slender, perfectly dressed, perfectly composed. She could spend a morning in the nursery and come out looking like a runway model. I would come out looking like Medusa on a bad-hair day.

I assumed at her house all the home-cooked meals were served on time, and the children sang songs from the "Sound of Music" before they went to sleep.

That's why I hardly recognized her when she came to my house one Tuesday morning.

Mascara streaked her face along with tears. Her hair was flat and lifeless. Her nose dripped on her T-shirt.

We sat down together on the couch and I asked her if she wanted to talk. Pouring out of her came a lifetime of hurt because of physical and verbal abuse. All of this culminated in the final betrayal. Her husband, a seasoned man of God, had been having an affair with a woman in the church, a trusted friend. "Why, Cathy? Why?"

My brain scanned all the platitudes, all the scriptures. Come on Holy Spirit, come on, brain, think of something spiritual, hopeful and comforting to say to her.

As I handed her another tissue, I patted her on the shoulder and muttered, "There, there. God will take this evil and turn it for His good." Oh brother! I knew I sounded stupid, trite and religious. Suddenly, as this precious woman of God was falling apart before me, I was very aware of my lack of ability to help her.

"Rejection!" I said it out loud, even as the Holy Spirit spoke it to me. "You are suffering a very deep wound of rejection."

As we prayed, she sobbed uncontrollably as God gave her a supernatural deliverance from a root of rejection. By the time she left, she felt clean, free and equipped to work out daily what the Lord had given to her that afternoon.

A key element that stops believers from fulfilling their destiny is inadequacy. It's a sense of inferiority that tells them that if they step out to do something by faith, they will be rejected.

The Faces of Rejection

One type of rejection is hostility. When you were in school, were you ever the last one chosen for a team because no one wanted you? To top it off, your team lost because of you. We carry many scars from childhood because of names like "four-eyes," "fatty-fatty two-by-four," "beanpole" or "Dumbo." Rejection is anything which makes us feel unloved, unwanted or unworthy.

After we come to Jesus, we are a brand new creation. Yet many Christians spend their entire lives trying to live down the images, words, wounds and pain inflicted on them while they were growing up. A person will either find acceptance in the Lord or he will try to gain it through his appearance, performance or possessions.

Years ago when I was in my teens, our church was packed for four nights in a row for a special series of meetings. We were experiencing revival. The worship and praise, the preacher and the altar ministry kept us returning night after night wanting more.

Now, I felt I was just as spiritual as anyone else in the congregation, and I wanted a glimpse of Jesus and the touch of the anointing as much as the others did. However, my eyes were fixed on the young evangelist, and I wanted a touch from him too!

After all, I was eighteen years old, and right here in our church was a real, live, young, good-looking *single* evangelist. And I could sing and play the piano, which everyone knows is a requirement to be an evangelist's wife. It was a sure sign from God. He had sent me a husband.

We fell in love, or lust, or whatever you want to call it, and the wedding date was set. Only one thing didn't seem right. The closer we got to the wedding day, the less I heard from him. Knowing and dreading the reality of what was happening, I did what most people who suffer from rejection do — I ignored it.

The invitation came a month before our wedding date. It was the invitation to celebrate his marriage to a girl he met in another church. Evidently, she played the piano and sang better than I did.

That did it! The wall went up, and I took an unholy vow saying, "I'll never let anyone hurt me that way again!" Yet, every time I heard the strains of "our song" or caught a glimpse of my veil sitting on the closet shelf in a box, my heart ached.

Rejection Will Destroy Your Self-Image

Rejection is a part of life. Jesus was rejected and despised, misunderstood, lied about, plotted against and finally murdered. It is amazing how many believers have even been deeply wounded by their Christian brothers and sisters.

The psalmist David said, "If it had been my enemies who betrayed me, I would have understood, but it was my personal friends who went into the house of God to worship with me that did it"(see Ps. 41:9).

Those who have been rejected are prone to pass along some form of rejection to those they love and are dearest to them. Satan uses an emotional bondage to rejection to continually try to cripple us. He sets us up to be rejected over and over and makes a fortress from which he can damage other people. He actually uses us.

When you come under a spirit of rejection, it sets you up to begin to do things that cause others to reject you. People under the influence of this spirit often decide the moment someone hurts them, "OK, buddy, you're off my list. I don't have to talk to you, and I will not have anything more to do with you."

This is repeated with each new relationship, until the person becomes a big island with no one around them. The spirit of rejection has isolated them. Those around them can readily sense their offense and self-pity.

In Luke 3:9, we find that almost all of our problems in life can be traced to the root of rejection that has never been dealt with. We must stop just lopping off the leaves and branches and go directly to the root. The tree — which includes fear, pain, lust, hurts, offenses and diseases — will die of natural causes.

Freedom for the Bruised

We find in Luke 4:18 that Jesus was mindful of those suffering rejection when He said He came "to set at liberty them that are bruised."

During His earthly ministry, Jesus knew healing would be a by-product of opening the prison door and setting the captives free. Today, when Jesus comes with the power of God's kingdom, He comes to pull down Satan's fortresses and set people free.

A person who has been rejected will ultimately reject himself and then others around him. They may say things such as, "If only I could be more spiritual. If only I could fast longer than half an hour. If I would pray more, be a better witness," and on and on they go with the "if onlys."

Unless you are set free from the spirit of rejection, you will never be able to relate to your Father in heaven. You will believe the lie of the enemy — that you can never please the Lord and you will never do anything right or good enough for Him.

All of us need to be loved. We want to be accepted just as we are — the good, the bad and the ugly — with our warts and all!

When we've been rejected, we react, in one way or another. In God's eyes, there's only one acceptable response to rejection, and it's found in Mark 11:25. That response is forgiveness.

Even if the transgression against us is severe, repeated or

totally unjustified, forgiveness is the only response God will accept. If forgiveness is withheld or even postponed ("I just need time to work through this by myself"), it provides an opening for the enemy to enter. He will seize upon every sinful reaction to the hurts of rejection.

The Evils of Rejection

Wrong reactions to rejection open doors to demonic activity. If we can identify the wrong reactions, we can shut the doors and keep them closed.

A wrong reaction will also cause us to lash out at others in confrontations of anger, bitterness and rebellion. It will cause self-pity, insecurity, fears and discouragement. Children are especially vulnerable to the wounds of rejection, which is why parents must guard their actions and words with love, prayer and discipline.

Let's look at the reactions rejection can produce.

1. Rebellion

If manifested, it develops into a hatred of authority. Rebellion will produce a tree with branches of self-will, independence, unteachability, stubbornness, defiance, selfishness and pride (see 1 Sam. 15:23).

2. Bitterness

It is an evil fruit, produced by one's unwillingness to forgive another his trespasses. It brings a curse of the tormentors. Many people live in "memory recall." They can push the rewind button of their minds and bring up events that happened years ago, events that have made them bitter.

3. Escapism

You just want to get away from it all. The circumstances of life turn sour and hurt you, so you devise ways of escaping. Daydreaming and sleeping can be a way of avoiding the responsibilities of life. Some people use drugs, alcohol and even television to numb their minds.

4. Self-pity

This inward reaction to rejection takes the form of self-affliction. You permit yourself to believe that people are unfair to you, and that will destroy your peace and joy.

5. Guilt

"I deserve the way I'm being treated. My problems are all my fault. This is a judgment from God." Many Christians live under this yoke of guilt as a result of living with someone who continually belittles them or blames them for everything that goes wrong. Remember, we have all blown it at some time in our lives, but our mistakes are all under the blood of Jesus now.

6. Inferiority or low self-esteem

You continually put yourself down to others. When you compare yourself with everyone else, you will always evaluate yourself as inadequate. You need to be aware of the fact that in God's eyes, no one is inferior. All He requires is faithfulness.

7. Insecurity

People who are not loved by those who they feel should love them are prone to doubt God's love. We see a picture and have an understanding of God's love from our earthly fathers. Sadly, in our society today, it is the exception and not the rule to find that healthy bond between a father and child. Rejected children become rejected adults who struggle with worry about everything from security to finances to favor with God.

8. Hopelessness

If you see no prospect of being loved you will become hopeless. That is why we must impart the love of Jesus to one another. Those who desire love should begin to pour out love to others.

9. Defensiveness

Defensiveness expresses itself in criticism and judgment of others. A person who judges begins to judge others who have hurt them and judged them. They can only see the faults of others, and they are prey to a spirit of deception.

10. Distrust

It's very difficult to trust and respect when wounded by rejection, betrayal, abandonment or unfaithfulness. Trust is destroyed and is followed by a destroyed relationship. Trust is not impossible to restore. However, it requires a great deal of humbling by the "wounder" and the grace of God to forgive by the wounded. At this point, hardness of heart will try to enter in.

Now that you know what rejection is, how it is allowed to come in and how to identify it, let me help you to be set free.

Respond, Not React

Reaction has to do with the soulish realm. Our mind, will and emotions are a part of the soul realm. There isn't anything evil inherent in this realm, for God created us with a mind in order to reason, think and remember. Our will makes choices for blessing and life, and our emotions make choices to feel love and righteous anger. However, when confronted with a

113

spiritual problem, we must respond through and with the Holy Spirit.

> Therefore all they that devour thee shall be devoured; and all thine adversaries, everyone of them, shall go into captivity; and they that spoil thee shall be a spoil, and all that prey upon thee will I give for a prey (Jer. 30:16).

This is an outrageous scripture to me, but I love it. Everything the devil did to you, Jesus is going to do to him through you. Captivate a demon and torment him? Awesome!

The God of peace will bruise Satan under your foot. In the same chapter, verse 17 says, "For I will restore health unto thee, and I will heal thee of thy wounds, saith the Lord; because they called thee an Outcast, saying, This is Zion, whom no man seeketh after."

Then the healing of the wounds comes. What wounds? The wounds of rejection.

You are chosen, loved, accepted and fit for the kingdom.

Prayer for Deliverance
From the Spirit of Rejection

Father, I come to You now, in the name of Your son Jesus, who loved me and gave Himself for me. I speak the blood of the Lamb of God over me and over my family.

I live in forgiveness. According to Matthew 18:23-35 I forgive from my heart, any and all, living and dead, who wounded me. I forgive them for knowingly or unknowingly rejecting me.

I forgive _____ for not loving me the way God intended for them to love me.

Lord, please forgive me for holding on to past

hurts, anger, unforgiveness or bitterness. I am released from any spirit and root of rejection, in the mighty name of Jesus. Go from me and return to the pit from where you came.

I thank You, Lord, for freedom and liberty. I thank You, Holy Spirit, for a fresh release of Your anointing and grace in my life. Keep me, Lord, in this fresh new walk. Amen.

11

If You Can Be Offended, You Will Be

The afternoon couldn't have started out any better. I was in Pittsburgh for a series of meetings, and several ladies from the area invited my mother and me out for lunch. They took us to a beautiful restaurant overlooking the city. I nibbled on a fresh salad topped off with a delicious, creamy garlic and onion dressing, while our hosts recounted to us the rich history of western Pennsylvania. Their stories brought back distant memories of high school. "Boy, I sure wish I had paid more attention in geography class so I could converse intelligently about this," I thought.

As we got into the car after lunch, I noticed a strong odor and thought, "Someone in this group really stinks. They need a breath freshener in the worst way."

I lowered the window and kind of stuck my nose out. I couldn't wait to get back to the hotel.

Once we arrived, I decided to rest a while before the next meeting. I took my dress off and was startled to discover that right there, nestled in my cleavage, was a piece of onion, slathered with garlic dressing. I said — out loud — "Oh my! It's me that stinks!" And all this time I thought it was somebody else.

I was offended by the smell in the car, when, lo and behold, it was me. That's what we usually discover when we step back and look at ourselves in situations of offense. When we get offended, we think it's always someone else's fault because they have (or have not) done something that we did not like.

Offense, the Fence of the Heart

Jesus said, "It is impossible that no offenses should come" (Luke 17:1, NKJV), meaning that every one of us will have a chance to be offended.

How do we get offended? Let me share a personal experience with you.

We once poured ourselves out in ministry to a particular family. We gave everything we had to give. When they stopped coming to church, I asked a mutual acquaintance why. I was told, "They said that you had failed them and offended them."

What? I mentally recounted all the things we had done for them. Among other things, we had invited them and their four children — they were expecting their fifth — along with their two nannies to live with us in our small two-bedroom house. Their intended one-week stay had stretched to two months. I was baffled; I thought we had been gracious to them.

A few weeks later, the mother of that family invited me out for lunch. I thought, "Good, she wants to apologize to me."

As we sat in the restaurant, she began, "I want to tell you this in love." I want to say something here. When someone starts a conversation with that phrase, brace yourself, because the next thing coming ain't love!

She began to tell me how I had offended her. I tried to smile, but the tears were stinging my eyes. As I listened, I thought, "God, right now, if You would, just come down and put a little bit of leprosy on her. Not a lot. Don't totally disfigure her, just a little around her jawline so she will know, bless God, she's wrong and I'm right."

Then I heard the Holy Spirit saying to me, "Do an Abigail."

Now Abigail was the wife of Nabal, a man who refused to help David and his men. So David set out to destroy Nabal (see 1 Sam. 25). Abigail found this out, prepared a peace offering and bowed down to David.

> When Abigail saw David, she quickly got off her donkey and bowed down before David with her face to the ground. She fell at his feet and said: "My lord, let the blame be on me alone. Please let your servant speak to you" (1 Sam. 25:23-24, NIV).

Abigail humbled herself, bowed low and found something to apologize for even though she wasn't responsible.

I was sitting there clenching my fist under the table, and the Lord said, "Just humble yourself and say you're sorry." So I obeyed and told her I was sorry that I hadn't realized I had offended her. I asked her to forgive me.

We prayed for restoration. When we parted she told me, "You may see us again. We just don't know what we're going to do right now." When I got into my car, the rewind tape of my brain started. I'm sure you have one too; that's the tape that sounds something like this: "Well, when she said this you should have said that. And what about the things her kids broke?"

I drove down the highway and wondered why I always think of witty things too late. I should have told *her* some things "in love"!

By the time I arrived home, I was loaded for bear. I told my husband I had just completely humiliated myself and recounted the confrontation to him.

Everyone needs someone to speak truth into their lives. God has given me that someone, the man I married. He looked at me and said, "Honey, you didn't humiliate yourself. You humbled yourself under the mighty hand of God, and He will exalt you."

My answer to him was, "Well, it was an accident, because I didn't mean to humble myself!" This precious family came back to the church as a direct result of my accidental humility! Eventually, we were able to sit down and talk openly and honestly in love, because they knew we would never throw them away.

Bounce Your Blessings Off Their Curses

Offense is evidence of iniquity in our hearts. It's not determined by the offense of the offender, but by our response.

Some of the most easily offended people are professional churchgoers. If you ask them where they go to church, they tell you they go wherever they are led. They're Christian cruise-o-matics. They leave one church because they got offended. Then they leave another because *you* got offended. Any excuse will do.

One Sunday morning when I was in charge of praise and worship, I was running late and rushed up to the keyboard. A woman later told me she had to ask the Lord to forgive me during communion. When I asked why, she said, "You rushed right by me and didn't even say good morning." I told her I was sorry, but my brain was screaming, "Get a life!"

You see how we get offended because other people get offended? When *we're* late, it's because we have so many responsibilities. When *they're* late, it's because they're self-important and inconsiderate. When *we're* irritable, it's because it's that time of the month. When *they're* irritable, it's because they're not exhibiting the fruit of the Spirit.

Spiritual jealously is another reason for offense. When others are blessed with something and we are not, jealously creeps in and we tend to become offended easily.

Randi and I once pastored a church in which we poured everything we had into it. We got two months behind on our house payment and were going to lose our home if God didn't intervene. All we needed to be current was two thousand dollars.

We were entertaining a lovely couple from another church one evening. I was carrying a plate of meatballs to the table when the wife said, "Did you hear? Someone just gave our pastor $300,000 to pay off his house." Needless to say, I almost dropped the meatballs in her lap. I answered something feeble like how wonderful that was and rushed back into the kitchen and cried, "Godddd!" I wanted to lift my fists up to Him and tell Him it wasn't fair.

I was jealous and offended because of the blessing that was poured out on that pastor.

In another church we pastored, my husband and I didn't go through a church split, we went through a church "left." The whole board resigned and left my husband and me with a great deal of debt. They bought a new building, moved the entire church there, and we didn't even know it.

One of our "allies" promised to stand by us; we'd rebuild and defeat the enemy that had infiltrated the church. But the other side offered them security, a car and more money. They abandoned us in a heartbeat.

When I heard this, I was at home in my bathrobe, and I just

slid down the side of the refrigerator and sat on the floor. At the time, if I could have just taken a deep breath and died, I would have. Have you ever felt like that?

I asked the Lord what to do. He said, "Just bless them." But you see, I didn't want to bless them, because I thought that if I blessed them, and then God blessed them, they would think that they were right all along.

I didn't want God to bless them. I wanted them to be cursed and shrivel up and die. The Lord again said, "Go to their building and bless them."

So I blessed them. Each night I stood outside their building and said, "Father, I forgive them; this is what I'm forgiving." I began to enumerate all the things I was forgiving them for.

I didn't feel like it at first. I was still angry. But I went back every night for thirty nights.

There are no words to describe what God did. The last night as I asked the Lord to bless them, minister to them, bring the lost to them, increase their finances and show them His glory, I meant every word that I prayed. I don't know how God did it; the hurt and the anger and the offense were totally gone.

A funny thing happens when you do what the Word tells you to do. The Word says to bless them that curse you. If you're speaking blessing and they're speaking curses, your blessing will come forth, bounce off of them and come back to you. Honey, if that doesn't stir you, your spoon is stuck to the side of the bowl!

Let Go, Monkey!

There are trappers in Africa who trap monkeys. They leave the gate on the front of a cage open, but the monkeys are too smart to go in the front.

Instead the monkeys reach from the side of the cage and grab the meat through the bars. The trappers are smarter and make the meat too large to fit through the bars. When a monkey tries to pull out the meat, it can't. It will screech and scream, but it won't let go.

The trapper walks up, knocks it on the head and has himself a monkey. The moral of the story — *Let go, monkey!*

The devil can get you if you are holding onto the bait (offense). If you let it go, the enemy can't get you. You need to pray to the Lord, "Father, I will not get offended. I refuse to be offended, and I let go of any offenses I might be harboring in my heart."

Some people are offended with everything and anything. "I don't like the way they take the offering." "I just don't like dancing in the church." In the light of eternity, what does it really matter? We *can* live our lives offense-free.

Remember Mary at Jesus' feet? She broke that alabaster box and people got offended. But Mary refused to get offended.

When you're sitting at the feet of Jesus, offenses just don't matter. Psalm 119:165 says, "Great peace have they which love thy law: and nothing shall offend them."

Maybe you have harbored offenses in your heart. You've been offended by parents, pastors, someone who got the recognition you felt you deserved, someone who didn't appreciate you.

But the Lord wants to deliver you and set you free. Do an Abigail. Bend, bow low, and say, "I'm sorry. Please forgive me." That breaks the flesh in us. It breaks the thing within us that wants to rise up and say, "It's not fair!"

Such humility pleases the Lord, because that's His nature and His Spirit. Release the offense and say, as Jesus did on the cross, "It doesn't matter. I'll take the blame."

12

Waiting for My Destiny While I'm Stuck in Suburbia

Growing up in church as a preacher's kid exposed me to every variety of church life. Some was God, some was, well...let's just say not God.

One time the Sunday school superintendent ate his picnic lunch on the roof of the church because we broke the attendance record. Not God — especially if he had lost his footing and fallen off the roof.

Several times a year we would have a missions Sunday. Definitely God. The missionary and his family, if he could afford to bring them (I secretly thought they were really at the mall), would stand on the platform in original native dress. White, pale, skinny missionaries in traditional deep jungle Katawabin tribal outfits. They looked ridiculous and probably felt that way, too.

However, sitting there on the front row of the church, we were in awe of these special people. They would sing a little missionary song in their native Katawabinish that would sound like:

> "Oh da kee
> We ataroachee
> Arnt yu gladu
> Duhnt haft ta go to."

We were shown many, many slides of the jungle church (click, click), the mission school (click, click) and people who had just accepted Jesus but who had no teeth (click, click).

I was enthralled! Not only did the sound of faraway places and fascinating stories of God's miracle power capture my little heart, but I knew there would also be no sermon to sit through.

The end of the service would always be the same. The missionary would have us reverently bow our heads and then ask who would be willing to go to the mission field for Jesus. No one moved! Of course no sane person wanted to leave their nice house, car, padded sofa with matching recliner and color television to live in a mud hut halfway around the world.

Who wants to sleep on a grass mat and eat eel entrails? Of course there was Eddie, who always raised his hand for everything, including the girls' softball team — but that's another story.

The missionary would then ask, "If you will not go, will you give in order that I may go?" This is what the crowd was waiting for and what the poor missionary was counting on. Hundreds of hands shot up all over the church. "Yes, I'll pledge five dollars a month so I can stay home on my recliner and not eat cream of locusts legs."

To say it was an emotionally charged moment was an understatement. Seriously, though, the problem was that we didn't understand that we really had a role to play in God's end-time harvest, and that God had a vision and a destiny for each of our lives.

We have heard many wonderful teachings, sermons, television programs, pastors and prophets challenge us to pursue a higher road. In fact, I believe we have no doubt heard, seen, read and forgotten more teaching than the rest of the world has yet to hear. But how many of us have a sense of destiny? How many understand our purpose in God?

Allow God's precious Holy Spirit to show you your destiny and purpose in your life. God desires to reveal who He is and what His purpose is in every situation of our lives.

> After these things I looked, and behold, a great multitude, which no one could count, from every nation and all tribes and peoples and tongues, standing before the throne and before the Lamb...and they cry out with a loud voice, saying, "Salvation to our God who sits on the throne, and to the Lamb."...and they fell on their faces before the throne and worshiped God saying "Amen, blessing and glory and wisdom and thanksgiving and honor and power and might, be to our God forever and ever" (Rev. 7:9-12, NAS).

Not only does God have a destiny for you, He has a destiny for all mankind. From the beginning of time He saw the day when He would be sitting on His throne and have a people from every tribe, nation, country and language who had been redeemed by the blood of His Son, Jesus, standing and worshipping before Him.

There are times you'll be waiting for your destiny and you'll feel overwhelmed. David wrote about this in a psalm.

> And I said, Oh that I had wings like a dove! for then would I fly away, and be at rest. Lo, then would I wander far off, and remain in the wilderness (Ps. 55:6-7).

I would love to rise up and fly, preferably before my next dental appointment and my four babies become teenagers and definitely before I've finished my forties.

There are about two thousand different people groups who have not yet heard the gospel. However, the Word declares there will be a representation from every tribe, people, nation and language. Do you see how the enemy has tried to shift our focus from reaching the lost to hanging on because we're glory-bound?

It doesn't matter if you're the firstborn, the last born, unwanted, adopted, young, old, in a wheelchair or bedridden, *you have a destiny in God.*

I know a very dear lady who was ill for a long time. When I last talked with her, she said she has been completely healed and is leaving for the mission field. She just celebrated her seventieth birthday.

My beloved grandmother, Ruth, is eighty-eight years old. She has been a widow for more than fifty years and doesn't get around like she used to. Because of nerve damage in her eye, she can't read. She still prays every day and fasts at least three days a month.

She said to me, "Cathy, I could have gone to be with the Lord years ago. I am tired, and it would be easier to go be with the Lord, but He told me I must stay and pray, that my work is not yet finished."

Your age doesn't matter when God has work for you to do. The most glorious words we will hear when we stand in His presence are: "Child, you have fulfilled your destiny to your generation. Well done, thou good and faithful servant. Come in, receive your crown and rest."

It may not be grand or glorious in the eyes of the world, but it's that kind of faithfulness and obedience that our God is looking for.

I know many precious people who never fulfill the will of God for their lives because they are continually getting healed. They've had twenty-five years of deliverance, inner healing, outer healing, counseling conferences and restoration! They've had everything cast out, cast in and overcast. Yet, they never come to the place where they allow God to flow through them, enabling them to touch the lost and hurting and become productive members in God's kingdom. The best way to see your vision come to pass is to help someone else bring theirs to pass.

The Church in Transition

We hear many Christian leaders say today that the church is in transition. Transition is when you're not where you used to be, and you're not where you're going to be, but you're stuck somewhere in between.

I compare transition to childbirth. When our first child Jerusha was born, my husband and I were so excited. We attended childbirth classes together, and I announced to everyone that I was not going to use any drugs. My child's birth was going to be completely natural.

I'm going to be like the women in China, I had told myself (and anyone else who would listen). I'm just going to bend down, drop that baby in the rice paddy, rinse it off and go on our way.

Shortly after I went to the hospital in labor, the nurse told me I had dilated one and a half centimeters. I thought, "Piece of cake. Only eight and a half more to go. I don't know what the big deal is — all those women on TV screaming."

The fun part comes at about six centimeters, when the baby is in transition — not in and not out. The baby is stuck somewhere in between.

At six centimeters I literally stood up on the bed and shouted, "I want morphine! I want cocaine! Give me a knife, I'll do it myself!"

My husband leaned down and began praying in tongues — something like, "Rondarasakayensitsmanayna." I looked at him and said, "Don't you rondarasakayensitsmanayna me. It's your fault to begin with. Get out!"

Do you remember how you felt when the nurse laid your firstborn in your arms? You said it was worth all the pain. Some women even went out and did it all over again!

Many Christians are in transition. They have a stack of unfulfilled words spoken to them by the Spirit of God. The words were true, but getting through the transition period was just too hard. They said, "I can't do it anymore" and gave up. They've tossed aside visions and dreams, prophecies and promises. Maybe you're one of those people.

When Self-Strength Dies

I had a dream to have more children. Those who have experienced any barrenness will understand the pain, longing and aching to hold that promise in your arms. "Just take the longing from me if You are not going to give me a child," I would cry over and over to the Lord.

I'd hear messages about standing and confessing a promise until the promise comes to pass. Later I'd hear a message about laying all of our "Isaacs" on the altar and surrendering them. I kept resurrecting my promise and then I'd put it on the altar and kill it. I honestly wasn't sure if I was to confess it or kill it. But the answer was...both! I had fallen into the trap that many believers do: I began to live for the promise instead of living for the Promiser.

Our attitude toward the enemy's attacks must be one of determined faith, confession and perseverance. Our attitude towards our heavenly Father must be one of total surrender and trust.

One day, after fifteen years of believing God for another child, the Lord spoke. "Daughter, I have a baby for you!" I said, "Please, Lord, don't tell me that again. I am just getting to the place of totally resting in You for another child."

Again I heard, "Daughter, I have a child for you. It is not a child that you will bear, but I will put a baby in your arms."

I cried a lot that day. I cried for what I thought at the time was disappointment, perhaps because my faith was not strong or perfect or unwavering. Although I knew I had shed tears of self-pity, I emerged from my prayer closet that day declaring, "Be it unto me according to Your will, because my life is not my own."

With those words, I washed my face and never told anyone of my encounter with the Lord.

A month later, a woman approached me at a meeting and handed me a business card. "If you would like a baby, we can place one in your home," she said. A week later, my husband and I were sitting in the adoption attorney's office, discussing the process. It was so unbelievable I thought I was going to have to pinch myself to see if I was awake. The promise was within our grasp.

Then the attorney said, "I will need a $6,000 retainer for court costs, the mother's living expenses, medical bills, etc." We didn't have $6,000. We didn't even have $600. My first reaction was to run out of his office and scream, "It's not fair, God, it's just not fair!"

My husband asked the attorney, "Will you accept a $2,000 retainer with a promise for the balance later?" Hearing him ask that question jolted me back to reality. The attorney agreed but would extend the time only by two days.

During the ride home, I did the natural "wife thing" and told Randi I didn't want to embarrass him in front of the attorney, but I thought it was important to remind him we didn't have $2,000. He reminded me of the words we often said, "God's will is God's bill."

Days passed and I began to panic. "Who can I call? Friends? No. Maybe we could sell our car? It's pretty hard to have a traveling ministry without a car. Bad idea." I called the adoption agency and begged them not to give away my baby.

Two weeks later I broke before the Lord. I fell to my knees and cried out, "I give up — again." He reminded me of the scripture I had been studying in Isaiah 6.

> In the year of King Uzziah's death, I saw the Lord sitting on the throne, lofty and exalted, with the train of His robe filling the temple. Seraphim stood above...
>
> And one called out to another and said, "holy, holy, holy, is the Lord of hosts, The whole earth is full of His glory" (vv. 1-3, NAS).
>
> Then I said, "Woe is me, for I am ruined! Because I am a man of unclean lips, And I live among a people of unclean lips;
>
> For my eyes have seen the King, the Lord of hosts."
>
> Then one of the seraphim flew to me, with a burning coal in his hand which he had taken from the altar with tongs. And he touched my mouth with it and said, "Behold, this has touched your lips; and your iniquity is taken away, and your sin is forgiven."
>
> Then I heard the voice of the Lord, saying, "Whom shall I send, and who will go for Us?" Then I said, "Here am I. Send me!" (vv. 5-8, NAS)

In Hebrew *Uzziah* means "the strength of Yahweh." It also means "God has helped." As Abraham did, there will come a time in our lives when we yield up the very promise of God in order to see His glory.

As I was sitting on the laundry room floor, the Lord spoke to me again and said, "Cathy, either you can do it or I can do it." I began to laugh and cry at the same time, realizing how foolish I had been. The Lord promised me this child, and I had decided He couldn't provide that child without my help.

My conversation with the Lord went like this: "Cathy, I have given you two weeks. How have you done?"

"Lord, I have fifty dollars, a pair of baby booties and a migraine headache."

God's answer, "Stand up, woman of God, praise Me for who I am. You are going to see a miracle. It is time."

He is the final authority, and only what He says matters. It does not matter what the circumstances may be, God wants you to arise and press in, and as you do, the circumstances will change.

Isaiah was not alone in the temple. There were priests and people worshipping, because there was never a time when the temple was totally empty. The Word says God came and revealed Himself. Even though the place was filled with people, Isaiah was the only one who saw His glory. Why? Because the others were preoccupied with death, greed and sorrow over King Uzziah.

If we do not listen for His voice or look for His glory in the middle of sorrow, suffering and pain, we may miss our destiny. Those are the places in which God desires to show Himself and speak to us. While others were grieving, Isaiah was worshipping the Lord in the year that Uzziah died. That's when Isaiah saw the Lord, and he spoke to Him.

In response to God's glory, Isaiah was filled with the sense of his own inadequacy. "Woe is me. I am a man of unclean lips. I'm undone."

The angel came with a hot coal. Cleansing comes, and God

speaks: "Who will go?" Isaiah said, like you and I must say, "Here am I, Lord, use me."

God did sovereignly provide finances for us within two days of my encounter with Him in the laundry room. Now, two years later, we not only have one blessing, we have five — our lovely natural teenage daughter, Jerusha Rose; a beautiful two-year-old black daughter, Hannah Ruth; biracial sons, Gabriel Levi also two, and Samuel Josiah, six weeks younger than Gabriel, and an infant daughter Abagael Elisha, who is also biracial.

Our four adopted children are not second best. Our love for them is equal to the love we have for our biological child.

God said He would have a people from every tribe, every nation, every tongue and every people. You don't necessarily have to go to them. The Lord may bring them to you!

A Prayer of Surrender

If you're frustrated, if you're tired of standing on the promises, if you feel the things God has promised will never come to pass, pray this honest prayer of surrender:

> Lord, I have done everything You have told me to do, plus about half a dozen more things You did not tell me to do. If I could have made the promise come to pass, I would have, because I've really tried. But right here, right now, I yield myself to your plan. Let me see Your glory. Let me hear Your voice. While I'm waiting, I will be Your missionary to a lost, dying and hurting world. Lord, my heart's desire is to fulfill my destiny that you have prepared for me. It is a destiny of hope, of blessing and being blessed, of giving mercy and grace, and enjoying your anointing, divine protection and direction. I trust You, Lord. I rest totally and completely in Your love for me. Amen!

13

You Can Be Cool, but Not of the Spirit

A local building supply company uses this slogan: "Don't move, improve." That can also apply to us spiritually.

We say we can't take it anymore. We'll just switch churches, spouses, jobs, houses, etc., and things will be better. Many Christians constantly move from church to church. They treat church like a spiritual cafeteria. What has become of covenant commitment?

The answer is not in moving. The answer is to improve the situation right where you are. The Lord wants to get His spiritual Roto-Rooter and begin to dig down deep in you so you can do His work and fulfill His purpose.

If the pastor gets on your nerves, ask the Spirit of God, "What are you saying to me through this man that makes me want to get out? What do You want to do in me?" The Spirit of the Lord is saying to you, "Don't move; don't run away; improve the situation right where you are with the anointing and with the tools of the Spirit."

Hold on to Your Anointing

The devil will try to steal your anointing. What's the anointing? The anointing is the supernatural power of God to perform something in word or deed that would be impossible for us to do in our own flesh.

The devil will try all different ways to take your anointing. His purpose is to steal, kill and destroy. You can be in a meeting where the presence of the Lord is so wonderful, and you leave walking on air. You get home and all it takes is one negative word from your spouse — boom! You're back in Gloomsville. I call it the transferring of spirits.

Invariably when I'm in a meeting, someone I don't know will want to pray for me. I am very careful who I allow to lay hands on me. There are some believers that I refer to as granola Christians: They're fruity, flaky and nutty, and I don't want their spirit on me.

One night, at the close of a message, I called for all those who needed prayer to come forward. When I looked up, standing before me was a really big guy with his arms folded in front of his body. He glared at me, and it was evident to me that he wasn't going to smile or move and that he was there to argue. I believe he thought God sent him there to straighten me out.

I did my best to be kind and asked him what he needed from the Lord. He said, "I'll tell you what. I don't agree with what's going on." I tried to pray for him, but he interrupted me and let me know he didn't approve. So I asked the Lord to let the power of God descend at that very moment.

God heard me. The next thing I knew, God's power came upon him, and in a flash he was lying prostrate on the floor with his arms still folded.

I can tell within thirty seconds if someone wants my counsel or if they want to argue with me. I have to depend on the anointing of God to deal with that. I don't have anything else. Those who want to argue the Word usually have a spirit of pride and arrogance, and if you are not careful, it will transfer to you.

Some women try to push the Lord on their husbands. They turn the television to a Christian channel and make sure the volume is up, or they put a preaching cassette in the car tape player so when their husband turns the motor on — bingo, instant evangelism!

Do you realize that if you walk in the anointing, you bring the very presence of the Lord into a room with you? That anointing will be imparted to those around you. It really works!

My grandmother, who has been around since Adam, has never preached at any public meeting, nor is she highly educated. But she can pray, and the power of God is so strong it will fill the room. That's the kind of anointing I'm talking about.

The enemy, though, will try to steal your anointing from you. He will use the negative comments of coworkers, relatives and friends to harass you. The man in Psalm 1 stays away from the counsel of the wicked. Don't allow the wicked to transfer a spirit of defeat on you! Hold on to your anointing.

Three Dog Night vs. Joy to the World

One way the devil will try to steal your anointing is through music. I was the speaker at a meeting in a hotel where other gatherings were taking place. As the women were in front singing praises and worshipping the Lord, the boom box in the next room was blaring a Three Dog Night song. I tried my best to minister, but I could tell the beat of the music was being transferred to our group.

As I moved from person to person to minister and pray for them, one woman was waving her hands and swaying as if lost in worship, but she was singing the words to a popular rock and roll song. She was not even aware of the influence of the music from the competing group next door. My first thought was, "Lord, one of us has got to go." My solution was to ask the praisers to sing louder than the music coming from the next room. It worked, and we had a mighty breakthrough that night as the Lord performed many miracles.

Music has an enormous influence on us. Do you remember the many times you have gone to church feeling discouraged? I have seen couples walk into the back of the church mad at each other over where one spouse chose to park. Then the worship begins to touch their spirit, and their hearts soften.

Where the Spirit of the Lord is present, the anointing will give you a release from the negative feelings you arrived with. It wasn't anything you did; it was simply the anointing. Remember, the anointing is caught, not taught. Surround yourself with people who walk in the anointing and in the Spirit of God.

Grocery and department stores understand the psychology of music. They play music in the background that says, "Stay a little longer. Buy a little more. Don't go home. Home is depressing. The shop-a-lot-and-you-will-save-a-lot place is where you want to be."

Once when I took my teenage daughter shopping, we found ourselves in a mall store that carried hideous clothing. My daughter went wild. Waiting for her to try on an outfit that resembled scuba diving gear, I started looking through the racks of clothing. Rock music was blaring through the store, and I noticed I was chewing my gum just a little louder than usual and swinging to the beat.

Before I knew it I had pulled out a pink leather miniskirt, lace tights and a pair of army boots for myself. My daughter said I looked like a poster child for a midlife crisis. "It was the music," I told her, my head hung in shame.

Now please, don't throw your cowboy boots at me, but country music has the same effect. Someone has either left, or they're coming back, or they're crying a tear in their beer from their ear over you. Not exactly edifying.

Fill your home, your car and your heart with His praise. When the psalmist David praised, his music drove the evil spirit from Saul (see 1 Sam. 16:23).

Computers Are Always Right, Aren't They?

There are all kinds of fear: fear of being in a tight place, fear of heights, of water, of failure, of losing your job, of losing your home...the list is endless. All fear, except the fear of the Lord, is from the devil and has to be treated as such. The enemy will use fear to steal your anointing.

I came home from a meeting one day to find I had an overdraft notice in my mailbox. To make matters worse, it was for my mortgage payment. I thought I was careful in my bookkeeping, but my concern now was how to break the news to my husband. According to my records, I had enough money in the bank. According to the bank, I was overdrawn $450. They should know. They have computers!

At the time, I was planning to buy groceries for a special Mother's Day dinner the following day. I began to get the kind of headache that starts in the back of my neck and works its way up. A terrible fear gripped my heart.

I couldn't buy the groceries because I had no cash, and I couldn't write another check. I called my mother — she and my dad were invited to dinner — told her the situation and canceled the dinner. She said she understood, which didn't make me feel any better.

I had planned to make chicken and yellow rice, using boneless chicken breasts. I sat on the floor and began to cry, asking the Lord to help me because, of course, none of this was my fault. But then again, computers don't lie, and the computer said *insufficient funds.*

Then came the proverbial knock at the door. No kidding! A knock at the door! When I opened the door, there stood a dear sister who said, "I don't know why, but I felt I just had to bring this bag over to you." When I asked her what was in it, she said, "Chicken breasts." I cried and she cried. Now I ask you, when was the last time you cried over chicken breasts?

I called my mom and said, "The dinner is on." Like He did with the manna, God rained chicken breasts.

The bank notified me a few days later that due to a transposition in the numbers, my deposit had been credited to someone else's account. The bank corrected their mistake, but I lost my confidence in computers.

The minute I begin to worry, the devil enters in. When I release my faith, God takes over. Fear brings Satan into a situation, but faith brings God into a situation.

Where's Your Motivation?

The third way the devil will try to steal your anointing is through passivity and complacency. You have no zeal for God, no energy, no motivation, and you feel as if you have been attacked by an evil spirit.

When the alarm goes off in the morning, the one that is signaling you that it's time to get up and pray, you push the snooze button. You've lost your fight; you're weary; you're tired of standing in faith. Beware of these signs of slothfulness, since you have become a certain target of the enemy.

No football game has been won just by the defense. The

players have to get their hands on the ball and run with it for a touchdown. Games are won with both defense and offense.

Have you ever prayed, "Oh God, I can't handle this situation anymore. If it isn't going to improve, just take me home to glory." God doesn't need you there, He wants you to fight right where you are. He has thousands of angels up there that do whatever He commands, and they don't complain or argue! He wants you to fight until the motivation and the anointing of the Holy Spirit comes.

On my second trip to the Philippines, we went to the island of Mindanao for a pastors' seminar. My parents were already there, and when I arrived they told me we had just enough time to get to the conference.

I was still in the same clothes I had traveled in for the past three days, and my first tendency was to complain. At the conference, there were over four hundred pastors and their wives crammed into a hot, stuffy room. They stood for an hour and a half, praising and worshipping God until the leader had to tell them to stop so we could minister the Word.

Suddenly, my attitude changed. I could just imagine people at home saying, "My feet hurt. We've been singing forever, and if she doesn't preach soon, I'll miss my TV show."

The only thing the Filipinos wanted to do was to improve the situation they were in. They had no transportation, no lovely homes, no beautiful clothes, but they had a zeal and love for God.

We tend to get complacent in our comfort, and it was in one of those times of complacency that the Lord showed me something rather odd. I was lying in my comfortable waterbed when I saw something "swoosh" past my eyes. It looked like a black blur.

I asked the Lord what it meant. He said, "It is a spirit of sloth that doesn't want you to pray." I got out of my comfortable bed, slid to my knees and asked Him to forgive me. I had succumbed to the spirit of passivity and complacency.

I won't tell you it was easy. For twenty minutes I walked the floor fighting that spirit. I walked to the front door, opened it, and commanded that spirit to leave. With great zeal I stood at the front door saying, "Out, out, I said you will go in the mighty name of Jesus! That's right — out of my house!"

I looked up to see my neighbor standing in his driveway, eyes wide, mouth open, watching me yelling at — nothing. I found out later he had backslidden in his faith. I must have scared him back into the kingdom of God.

Satan's purpose is to make you give in to your lethargy. I believe the apostles were dealing with the spirit of sloth when they couldn't stay awake to pray with Jesus in the garden the night of His arrest (see Luke 22:39-46). Satan doesn't want you to improve; he wants you to move and be miserable somewhere else. Don't stop! Get back into the fight and don't stop until the release comes.

You Can Be Cool, but Not of the Spirit

In Revelation 3:14-16 we read, "I know your deeds, that you are neither cold nor hot; I would that you were cold or hot. So because you are lukewarm, and neither hot nor cold, I will spit You out of my mouth" (NAS). That's strong stuff.

Coolness of spirit will steal your anointing, but not all at once. It happens gradually. We are lulled into passivity when we don't pray as often as we used to. Church attendance becomes erratic, and we believe the lies of the enemy. Our willingness to fight has decreased. We want to do our own thing. Rebellion creeps in.

When you get up in the morning, clap your hands and say, "Devil, draw nigh; I have a word for you." Don't wait for him to find you. Say, "I declare to you that every plan you have against me or my family will not prosper; I speak confusion to you and your camp."

Be like Rambo. Tell the devil, "I'm your worst nightmare."

When you are wrapped in the robes of the righteousness of the Lord Jesus Christ, you have the power of God in your life.

I have a treadmill that I get the urge to blow up at times. It's one of those things that I just had to have, but it doesn't do me any good if I just stand and stare at it. It just stares back, making me feel guilty. Then there was the stationary bike I had to have, and the trampoline I thought would solve all my problems. Three minutes on any of them, and I start gasping for air.

If I don't use any of these gadgets, they won't do me any good. But I had to learn that I couldn't expect to go for an hour at first. I had to build up my endurance.

Go the Distance

I have always admired marathon runners. If, and that's a big IF, I could ever manage to run a marathon, I would have to be carried across the finish line on a stretcher, hooked up to an oxygen tank.

But an Olympic runner needs no help. The winner enters the Olympic stadium to the deafening roar of the crowd. Instead of collapsing at the finish line, the winner continues to run, taking an additional victory lap around the track!

Why is the crowd cheering? He's accomplished something they couldn't do. He was well-trained to do what he did, but he started out a little at a time, ending with the victory lap.

When we begin exercising our faith muscles, we may pray only five minutes a day. As is the case when we use exercise equipment, we must build up our endurance.

Fight passivity with boiling hot prayers against the enemy. Invest your life in praise and prayer and a church life. Reach for a greater measure of God's anointing than you ever had before.

I heard a story about "the greatest fight of all time" that really ministered to me (maybe because I've felt like a punching bag so many times). This fight took place between Muhammad Ali and Joe Frazier in the Philippines.

Frazier kept hitting Ali again and again, and both were bleeding all over the ring. (Sounds pretty gross, huh?) Ali didn't give up though. He kept getting back in Frazier's face to fight some more. Neither boxer ever went down, instead they kept pummelling each other until both were beat, cut up and swollen. Finally, after round fourteen Joe Frazier refused to come out of his corner. Ali won the fight.

When the enemy keeps trying to beat you, keep getting back in his face and let him have it. Eventually, he'll refuse to come out of his corner.

Jesus Christ stepped into the boxing ring and took a pounding for us when He died on the cross. We can take a beating and still be a winner. Jesus is the conqueror, and you are the "more than a conqueror" because through Him you obtain the prize.

The Spirit of God speaks to you and tells you, "Don't move, improve." Endure the attack. Don't look for a new word. Take the word you have, and begin to believe that what God said, He will do!

14

What Do You Mean, There's No More Manna?

I was in a meeting when the Lord spoke to me about a woman who sat about two-thirds of the way back in a large crowd. He gave me a song for her. Through that song, He said He was taking her out of grief and turning mourning and darkness into joy and rejoicing. Among other prophetic words, He told her that her husband was going to rise up, and God was going to use him in medical missions.

She later told me that her husband was a doctor. She said, "You don't know what that word has done for us." She and I rejoiced in the Spirit of God, and how precise God is.

Why does He do that?

The word of the Lord comes forth to give us something to fight the devil with. It empowers us to do warfare against doubt. On the other hand, we need to become so confident in who God is that even when we don't understand exactly what He's doing, we trust that He's doing it right.

Where's Your Squealing Point?

One Thursday, God did a tremendous thing for me. He moved miraculously to meet a great financial need. But the following Monday morning, things were not looking so tremendous.

I had awakened to the sound of rushing water. That would have been all right, except for the fact that it was four in the morning, and no one was in the shower. I got up and looked everywhere to find out where the sound was coming from. I finally went into the garage and saw water cascading everywhere.

I found the main water valve to the house, managed to turn it off and decided to call the plumber when it was more affordable. It soon became evident that like it or not, "more affordable" was *now*. But even the plumber couldn't find the leak right away.

Several hours later he came in from the garage all sweaty (that's always a sure sign it is going to cost big bucks). He told me the leak was in the cement underneath the water heater. He said he'd have to break up the cement.

I thought, "Great, we're not going to have water for a month, so get used to it." To make matters worse, I discovered the toilet had overflowed and flooded my bedroom and closet. The aroma was something else! It was a mess. We had to haul water, and the place smelled so awful that I became depressed and looked for someone to blame.

My husband was in Russia at the time. When he called, my

immediate thought was, "Good — now I have someone to blame." I began to cry and told him he should have been home, because, after all, this was a man thing. "I don't know how I'm going to pay the plumber," and on and on I cried.

After listening to me wail for a while, he said, "Honey, I can't believe you. You are guilty of the sin of the children of Israel."

For one second I had a very clear notion to hang up on him. After it passed, I asked, "Well, exactly how many children of Israel? All of them, or maybe three or four?"

He reminded me how the children of Israel started complaining and worrying about the food supply only two and a half months after God parted the Red Sea so they could walk through on dry ground (see Ex. 16:1). God had moved so phenomenally that previous Thursday, and here it was only Monday and I was already grumbling and complaining. I was *worse* than the Israelites. The Holy Spirit pricked my heart as my husband continued, "I'm sorry I wasn't there, but the Lord let this happen because He wanted to see what was in your heart. He wanted to see your squealing point."

At that point I didn't know whether to squeal at him, "You just don't understand!" or go ahead and repent. When faced with a crisis, our natural instinct is to tell someone our problem in order to get their sympathy, when what we really need is someone who will challenge our spirit and not just stroke our flesh.

I told Randi he was right, and I stood convicted. After I hung up, I fell on my face and repented before the Lord. You see, I hadn't even realized what was in my heart. As soon as the devil attacked me, what was in me came squishing out — and I didn't like what I saw.

When the children of Israel complained to God, "You brought us all out here and we are going to starve to death." He responded, "I will rain bread from heaven for you" (see Ex. 16:14).

God caused manna to rain down from heaven. The Lord instructed the people to go out each day and gather enough for that day. He was testing them to see if they would follow His instructions. He gave them provision on a day-to-day basis.

Manna is God's base provision for you. Manna is God's mercy to you. We get all excited about manna. We sing songs about manna.

Manna is all right, but it is just a temporary diet, not the food we're supposed to live on permanently. It would keep the Israelites alive — but it certainly wasn't meat and potatoes. You want more out of life than just being alive; you want meat and potatoes.

I once was involved in a well-known weight-loss program. The leaders told us, "When you're hungry, get some rice cakes." Have you ever tasted rice cakes? To me they taste like compressed pieces of cardboard, held together with Elmer's glue. That, along with two ounces of plain yogurt and four ounces of skim milk, was supposed to suppress the gnawing in my stomach. But that's not what I wanted. I wanted a big chocolate candy bar.

Even though manna was sweet to taste, I think that forty years of anything would begin to stick in your throat. Some of you are sick and tired of the same old thing. That's OK. God wants you so sick and tired of being sick and tired that you will do something about it.

I have a saying: "If you always do what you've always done, you'll have what you have right now." God wants to move us into reckless faith. Tell God, "I know that where You guide, You provide."

Keep on "Driving"

As the children of Israel reached the border of the land God promised them, they were directed to send twelve spies into the country (see Num. 13-14). One man from each of the twelve tribes was chosen. They traveled for forty days, seeing everything and everyone in order to bring back a report to the people.

Straining under the load of heavy grapes and fruits of this promised land "flowing with milk and honey," all but two of the spies brought a negative report. "There are giants so large living there. We are like grasshoppers in their sight. They live in walled cities we cannot possibly fight against," (v. 33) the ten reported.

Joshua and Caleb were the only two who believed they should obey God and enter the promised land immediately. They tried to convince the people to act on faith, but the Israelites would not listen.

As often happens when faith is absent, grumbling and complaining began. God became angry because of their lack of faith and obedience. Finally, God swore that none of those who were considered adults would ever set foot in the promised land. They would spend the next forty years wandering around in circles until they were all dead.

The ten spies who brought the bad report and caused the Israelites to grumble were immediately struck by a plague and died. They didn't even get a forty-year reprieve.

God is a merciful God. He tolerates our immaturity, but there comes a time when we must reach maturity in Christ. If we do not — if we don't fulfill our destiny and don't walk in the things the Spirit of God has for us — then He will give that destiny to someone else.

A Christian publisher invited me to speak to his staff. He said, "God wants to raise up a people with a *now* word for His body. Would you please come and share a *now* word with us?"

I thought about it for a long time — well, as long as it took to drive to the meeting. I told the Lord, "I've got to have a *now* word and I need it *now!*"

The Lord said to me, "A now word is simply what I am doing in the earth today." Just that simple but beautiful. It's no big secret. You don't have to study fifteen translations of the Bible and spend ten hours in prayer every day. Just get into the presence of the Lord and ask Him to speak through you. Have you been fighting, struggling with your job, finances, depression? You're living on manna, which is temporary.

Moses dragged the children of Israel through the wilderness, but Joshua drove them into the promised land. They got sick and tired of being sick and tired and made the decision to go in.

You may be the one that has to stand in faith for your family, but I encourage you to keep on "driving." When the Israelites reached the Jordan, they put their foot in and the waters parted. They went across on dry land. You may be closer to your "dry land" than you think.

We often sing songs that ask God to melt us, mold us, break us, fill us — and what does God do? He puts us in situations that do just that. I can just see the angel when God is ready to melt us. He tells him to turn up the fire. It's so hot the angel has to use tongs; then he applies the heat. And we begin to cry, "I bind that, I bind that!" All God is doing is what you asked Him to. He's burning off the old flesh. Then He can mold us into what He wants us to become.

It's painful. I would love to tell you that God will just take you all to Disney World and let you have a hilarious time, but that's not how it works.

When the children of Israel reached Canaan, the manna stopped appearing each morning. They had reached the land flowing with milk and honey. Was the milk flowing down in waterfalls off the mountaintops? No. Where was the milk? In the cow, of course.

"That's just great. Now I've got to put up with these flies and sit here and milk this cow." And how about the honey? "In the beehive? I thought it would just be there. I just know I'm going to get stung."

It's never the way we thought it was going to be, is it? It was always a lot easier in the tent. Just lift up the old flap while everyone is comfy in their sleeping bags, scrape in some manna and feed the whole family.

It never ceases to amaze me how many precious believers are content living in the wilderness with only "manna" to sustain them. After a season, manna became boring and the children of Israel became discontent and wanted more. They tried to get God's attention by murmuring and whining.

It is still the same today. As long as our needs are met, we become complacent and our faith is never really challenged.

Three million Israelites complained while one man, Moses, prayed. God heard and moved because of that one man. Believe me, I know from experience that complaining gets you nowhere with God.

The Word says, "The Lord inhabits the praises of His people." Who is it that inhabits the complaining of His people? Whining brings the enemy into our situation while praising brings God into action in our situation.

If you have lost hope for your need, problem or situation, the Lord has good news for you:

1. Return to the place of total surrender.

2. Begin to verbally praise and thank Him.

3. Think of your loving Father, not only as your provider but also as your provision.

He is not only your bread *for* life, He is the bread *of* life!

Epilogue

One of the questions I am often asked is, "When and how did you first begin to use the gift of prophecy?" I remember it as if it were yesterday.

I sat at the piano, softly playing background music while Randi ministered to people. He looked over and said, "Honey, the Spirit of the Lord has come upon you to prophesy. Come here and deliver what the Lord is saying." Totally mortified, I looked at him and tried to appear spiritual. With a faint smile I shook my head, said, "No, I don't have anything," and kept on playing.

He repeated, "Come and deliver what the Holy Spirit is telling you." I stood up with tears flowing down my cheeks and walked to where he was standing. I will tell you frankly, these were not tears from the Holy Spirit. I was crying out of embarrassment and humiliation because the last thing I wanted to do was to prophesy to some poor unsuspecting soul. But Randi called a dear sister up from the congregation, turned to me and said, "Prophesy the word of the Lord to her."

At that moment I knew that if I went before a judge and told him, "My husband made me prophesy when I didn't want to," he would immediately grant me a divorce. However, there was no way out, so I began to pray in the Spirit and began to, uh, prophesy.

"The Lord says that either in the past or in the future or now, I have either moved for you, will move for you or I am moving for you."

With that profound statement, I went back and sat down at the piano. My husband looked at me and said, "No, come back. I believe the Lord desires to speak to her about her husband." If looks could kill, he would have been lying flat on that platform. I thought, "I'll have a word or two for him when we get home." But I knew I had better go back and do what he said.

I asked the woman, "Are you married?"

"No," she replied.

So I said, "God is going to give you a husband." When I sat down she began to shout and rejoice.

That was my first prophetic word over someone. (Thankfully, since that time God has graciously increased His anointing on me and has fine-tuned His gift in my life.) Can you imagine my surprise when I received a letter from her six months after that prophecy saying she got married?

When we begin to speak out what we sense God is saying to someone, faith is released in that person's life. Faith gives them hope, and hope gives them the power to wait until God's promise is fulfilled.

Because of the tests and trials I have faced and overcome I feel a greater measure of anointing on my life. But the demand of marriage, motherhood and ministry are never ending. There will always be a stack of laundry, a child needing attention, a sinkful of dishes, a demanding job, a hungry family to feed, or in my case a plane to catch. But my question is this: Where are our priorities?

The Lord understands you must have the hands of Martha to accomplish all of these tasks. However, what's more important is that you have the heart of Mary. It pleases the Father and fills His heart when you sit at His feet and spend time with Him.

It was when I began to follow this principle that the Lord turned my "Crete" into my crown, and my misery became my ministry. God turned everything around for me when the enemy kept telling me, "How can God bring this to pass?" But the Holy Spirit urged me to press on and hold onto His promises. I did and I won.

I believe God will set you free and release joy within you. He will fulfill your destiny. His words to you will come to pass if you wait and let Him move for you. Don't be anxious and expect everything to happen overnight because it's not that easy. But God does have a plan for you, and just when you think you can't hang on any longer remember that victory is one step beyond the faint. Press on and you will win!